T0323611

Cambridge Elements ≡

Elements in the Problems of God
edited by
Michael L. Peterson
Asbury Theological Seminary

GOD AND HAPPINESS

Matthew Shea
Franciscan University of Steubenville

CAMBRIDGE
UNIVERSITY PRESS

Shaftesbury Road, Cambridge CB2 8EA, United Kingdom

One Liberty Plaza, 20th Floor, New York, NY 10006, USA

477 Williamstown Road, Port Melbourne, VIC 3207, Australia

314–321, 3rd Floor, Plot 3, Splendor Forum, Jasola District Centre,
New Delhi – 110025, India

103 Penang Road, #05–06/07, Visioncrest Commercial, Singapore 238467

Cambridge University Press is part of Cambridge University Press & Assessment,
a department of the University of Cambridge.

We share the University's mission to contribute to society through the pursuit of
education, learning and research at the highest international levels of excellence.

www.cambridge.org
Information on this title: www.cambridge.org/9781009517164

DOI: 10.1017/9781009270182

First published 2024

A catalogue record for this publication is available from the British Library.

ISBN 978-1-009-51716-4 Hardback
ISBN 978-1-009-27020-5 Paperback
ISSN 2754-8724 (online)
ISSN 2754-8716 (print)

Cambridge University Press & Assessment has no responsibility for the persistence
or accuracy of URLs for external or third-party internet websites referred to in this
publication and does not guarantee that any content on such websites is, or will
remain, accurate or appropriate.

God and Happiness

Elements in the Problems of God

DOI: 10.1017/9781009270182
First published online. December 2024

Matthew Shea
Franciscan University of Steubenville

Author for correspondence: Matthew Shea, MShea@franciscan.edu

Abstract: This Element explores the connection between God and happiness, with happiness understood as a life of well-being or flourishing that goes well for the one living it. It provides a historical and contemporary survey of philosophical questions, theories, and debates about happiness, and it asks how they should be answered and evaluated from a theistic perspective. The central topics it covers are the nature of happiness (what is it?), the content of happiness (what are the constituents of a happy life?), the structure of happiness (is there a hierarchy of goods?), and the possibility of happiness (can we be happy?). It argues that God's existence has significant, positive, and desirable implications for human happiness.

Keywords: happiness, well-being, God, theism, morality and religion

ISBNs: 9781009517164 (HB), 9781009270205 (PB), 9781009270182 (OC)
ISSNs: 2754-8724 (online), 2754-8716 (print)

Contents

1 The Concept of Happiness

1.1 The Universal Desire for Happiness

Plato says that philosophy begins with wonder (1990: 155d). He is right about that. But philosophy can also begin with platitudes. Here is one that, when subjected to reflection, can produce great wonder: *Everyone wants to be happy*. This fact about human nature has been acknowledged by many of the leading thinkers throughout the ages. Plato, representing the mainstream view among the ancient Greeks, says, "[there is no] need to ask why a man desires happiness; the answer is already final" (1956: 205a). His disciple Aristotle observes that "Verbally there is very general agreement [about the final end and highest good of human life]; for both the general run of men and people of superior refinement say that it is happiness, and identify living well and faring well with being happy" (1984: Bk. I, 1095a). According to the Roman Stoic Cicero, "The entire end and aim of philosophy is the attainment of happiness; and desire for happiness is the sole motive that has led men to engage in this study" (1931: 177). His fellow Stoic Seneca claims that "To live happily ... is the desire of all men" (2007: 41). Echoing him, the ancient Christian philosopher and theologian Augustine of Hippo writes that "We all certainly desire to live happily; and there is no human being but assents to this statement almost before it is made" (1887b: Ch. 3).

Medieval thinkers affirmed the same position. Boethius expresses it like this: "All anxieties of mortal men, driven on by the exertions of uncountably diverse pursuits, travel along paths that are, to be sure, quite different; yet they all strive to reach only one single goal: true happiness" (2001: Bk. III, Prose 2). According to Anselm of Canterbury, the desire for happiness is a natural and inescapable inclination of the human will (2007b). For Thomas Aquinas, "man's last end is happiness, which all men desire" (1920: I-II, q. 1, a. 8), and "man must, of necessity, desire all, whatsoever he desires, for the last end" (1920: I-II, q. 1, a. 6).

The view that everyone desires happiness persisted into the modern period. According to Joseph Butler, "Every man hath a general desire of his own happiness" (1983: 47). Immanuel Kant says, "There is one end that can be presupposed as actual in all rational beings ... and that is the purpose of happiness" (2012: 4, 415). Going a step further, John Stuart Mill claims that "Each person, so far as he believes it to be attainable, desires his own happiness ... .[H]uman nature is so constituted as to desire nothing which is not either a part of happiness or a means of happiness" (2001: 35, 39). And Blaise Pascal memorably writes:

> All men seek happiness. There are no exceptions. However different the
> means they may employ, they all strive towards this goal. The reason why
> some go to war and some do not is the same desire in both, but interpreted in
> two different ways. The will never takes the least step except to that end.
> This is the motive of every act of every man, including those who go and hang
> themselves. (1995: No. 148)

In our own age, happiness-talk is ubiquitous in our public and private discourse, and there is an enormous amount of interest in happiness among academics, administrators, advertisers, policymakers, health professionals, self-help gurus, and the general population. According to a recent *World Happiness Report*, an annual study of global happiness, references to happiness in printed media have risen dramatically over the past several decades. Since 1995, the use of the term "happiness" has steadily increased across all studied languages; "the frequency of use of 'happiness,' as a fraction of all text in books, has more than doubled, while that of 'subjective well-being' has increased by a factor of eight" (Barrington-Leigh 2022: 56). Furthermore, "there has been more than a 10-fold increase in research output on happiness since the turn of the century" (Barrington-Leigh 2022: 55). These international trends attest to the universal longing for happiness.

In claiming that everyone longs to be happy, my point is not that everyone agrees about what happiness is and how it is achieved. Clearly, they do not. Instead, our starting point is the observation that all human beings want to live a happy life. As Aristotle puts it, "living well and doing well" is something that all of us naturally care about, desire, and pursue. It is no surprise, then, that happiness is a perennial source of wonder and philosophical reflection. Every major intellectual tradition speaks to the question of happiness, and many of them hold that happiness is one of the highest – if not the very highest – values, ends, and priorities in life.

Now consider what Pascal says next:

> Yet for very many years no one without faith has ever reached the goal at which
> everyone is continually aiming. All men complain: princes, subjects, nobles,
> commoners, old, young, strong, weak, learned, ignorant, healthy, sick, in every
> country, at every time, of all ages, and all conditions ... What else does this
> craving, and this helplessness proclaim but that there was once in man a true
> happiness, of which all that now remains is the empty print and trace? This he
> tries in vain to fill with everything around him, seeking in things that are not
> there the help he cannot find in those that are, though none can help, since this
> infinite abyss can be filled only with an infinite and immutable object; in other
> words, by God himself. (1995: No. 148)

Pascal thinks that true happiness is found in God. This is another doctrine that has been affirmed from antiquity until our own time. For Plato, supreme happiness consists in being like God, and this should be the goal of our earthly striving: "A man should make all haste to escape from earth to heaven; and escape means becoming as like God as possible . . . .[T]here are two patterns set up in reality. One is divine and supremely happy; the other has nothing of God in it and is the pattern of the deepest unhappiness" (1990. 176a5–e4). The most famous expression of the idea that happiness is found in God comes from Augustine, when he says to God: "Thou hast made us for Thyself, and our hearts are restless till they rest in Thee" (2006: Bk. I, Ch. 1).

1.2 Happiness

Now, one question that immediately arises is: What does "happiness" mean in the first place? What are these authors referring to when they talk about happiness? It is not safe to assume they have the same thing in mind, and in some cases it is clear they do not. The question "What is happiness?" can be taken in two different ways. The first is to ask for the definition of the word "happiness" and the meaning of the concept *happiness*. The second is to ask about the nature of happiness itself. We will address the first question now and the second question in the next section.

One of the challenges in discussing happiness is that it has a wide range of meanings in popular usage, history, and philosophy. The concept of happiness that I will use throughout this Element is the classical one that corresponds to what contemporary philosophers often call "well-being," "welfare," or "flour-ishing." It does not mean being happy in the sense of having a cheerful personality or feeling subjectively content. Instead, it means leading a happy life. It is not an emotion or mood, but a state or way of living.

A key feature of happiness (in my sense) is that it is a *normative* concept: it does not describe a person's psychological state; it *evaluates* a person's life as being good or bad. A different and popular sense of happiness takes it to be a state of mind like subjective satisfaction or positive emotions and feelings, a purely descriptive psychological condition that is not value laden. By contrast, happiness in my sense is a *good*: something that has positive value and is desirable and worthy of pursuit, promotion, and protection. To be more precise, it picks out one of the main ways that we evaluate a human life. When we think about the different ways a life can be good, there are various goods that contribute to its overall goodness. Some of the major ones are happiness, morality, beauty, knowledge, dignity, meaning, and excellence. Philosophers disagree about whether these goods are fundamental kinds of value, whether certain ones can be reduced to others, and how they are connected. These axiological disputes need not concern us here, because the various goods are at least formally and conceptually distinct (even if not substantively and metaphysically distinct), and the one we are focusing on is happiness.[1]

Happiness is one specific kind of goodness, which is usually called *prudential value* or *goodness-for*. It is what's intrinsically or non-instrumentally good *for* an individual, benefits her, and makes her life go well for her. Richard Taylor defines it as the state of "having achieved fulfillment or having been blessed with the highest personal good . . . the kind of good that normally takes the better part of a lifetime to attain" (2002: 111). Happiness is typically contrasted with *intrinsic value simpliciter*: goodness that is not good for anyone or anything, just "good period"; something that makes the world a better place even if it has no relation to any individual. Happiness is also conceptually distinct from *moral value*: acting in accordance with moral obligation, having a morally admirable character, and so on. It may be the case that moral goodness is also good for someone, but this is not a conceptual truth. Finally, happiness should not be confused with an *overall good life*: a broader notion that signifies a life that is desirable or choice-worthy on the whole, not just morally good or good for an individual, but good all things considered, taking into account all the goods that contribute to the total value of a life. Some thinkers, especially Aristotle and his followers, are often interpreted as equating happiness with an overall good life; but I will operate with the narrower notion of happiness in this work.

Philosophical theories of happiness can target either *lifetime happiness* – the happiness of a whole life, how well a person's life goes overall – or *momentary happiness* – the happiness of a particular episode or phase of life, how well a person's life is going at some moment in time. They are connected, and both will be explored in this Element. My typical focus will be lifetime happiness because it matters more. Julia Annas notes that "As we bring up our children, what we aim for is not that they have episodes of smiley-face feeling, but that their lives go well as wholes: we come to think of happiness as the way a life as a whole goes well, and see that episodes of happiness are not what we build our lives around" (2004: 45).

Throughout this Element, I will use "happiness" in the sense outlined above, and it will be important to keep this definition and concept in mind. (Sometimes the terms "well-being" and "flourishing" will be used interchangeably with "happiness.") It is clear that happiness is part of a good life and is something we

---

[1] For helpful overviews of the concept of happiness/well-being as I am construing it, see Haybron (2013); Fletcher (2016: Ch. 1); Heathwood (2021: Ch. 1). Although these authors, like most contemporary philosophers, prefer the term "well-being," I think that "happiness" is acceptable and perhaps preferable because it is more commonly used in the history of philosophy and in ordinary discourse.

desire for ourselves and for the people we care about. Happiness matters to us all. This means that if the theistic philosophers are right that God matters for happiness, then God should matter to us too.

1.3 Overview

The proposition that God is the source and summit of true happiness is affirmed by many of the great philosophical traditions and by the three major monotheistic religions of Judaism, Christianity, and Islam, as well as other religious traditions. And yet, in recent philosophy, theistic conceptions of happiness have received much less attention than they deserve. As Hud Hudson observes, "In surprisingly many of the contemporary prominent discussions of well-being and happiness, religious topics in general (much less something as specific as one's relation with God) tend to be rather thinly represented or to get a half-hearted nod by way of reference to broadly spiritual beliefs, attitudes, and practices" (2021: 80). This neglect is unfortunate not only because many people's view of happiness includes God, but also because theism casts the traditional philosophical problems of happiness in a new light and raises a host of interesting and important questions. The most basic one is, "What does God have to do with happiness?" Many people today will be tempted to answer this question with "Nothing," or perhaps with "Something, but only for those who are religious or who believe in God." I will argue that the correct answer is "A lot": God's existence (or non-existence) is very significant for human happiness, and this is relevant to everyone, not just religious people or theists.

Robert Adams suggests that "if theism can be commended persuasively to our modern minds, it will be in large part through the felicity of the contribution it can make to our treatment of such topics of common concern" (1999: 5). Happiness is certainly one such topic. When we analyze and evaluate philosophical positions, theories, or worldviews, one important question we should ask is how they bear on the things we care about. All of us care about happiness, both our own and that of the people we love. Indeed, a very old and popular tradition in philosophy, represented by some of the authors quoted earlier, says that personal happiness is something that everyone *necessarily* wants and pursues as their *single final end* in life, which governs *all* of their (rational) desires, motives, choices, and actions. On this view of practical reasoning, all the other ends we pursue are ultimately for the sake of our own happiness. Whether or not this is true, happiness matters a great deal to all of us, which means that God's existence matters for something we all care about. Because one test of a worldview should be how it bears, both theoretically and practically, on human happiness, the consequences of theism for happiness should be an important factor when we evaluate it as a worldview.

The goal of this Element is to explore the implications of theism for some central philosophical problems concerning happiness. Although the study of happiness is multidisciplinary – spanning philosophy, theology, psychology, economics, and other fields – my approach will be philosophical, drawing upon reason and common human experience. The overarching inquiry running throughout the volume can be summarized as follows: Does God's existence make a difference for human happiness? When it comes to our understanding and pursuit of happiness, does God matter? The overarching answer and theme of the volume is: Yes, God matters a great deal for human happiness. I will argue that theism provides answers to some of the most important questions we can ask, and it has significant theoretical and practical implications for our happiness. One of these philosophical questions, which we have already answered, concerns the *concept of happiness*. The three other main questions addressed in this Element are the *nature of happiness* – what is it? (Section 2), the *content and structure of happiness* – what are the constituents of a happy life, and is there any hierarchy among them? (Section 3), and the *possibility of happiness* – can we attain it? (Section 4).

When answering these questions, there are two different methods that one might adopt. The first, which we can call the "bottom-up" method, is to begin with a specific theory of happiness and then see how God fits into that framework. This is the standard approach in the philosophical literature. The second, "top-down" method reverses the direction of analysis by starting with a conception of God and asking what it means for human happiness. This will be my method. I will begin with theism and consider the problems of happiness from a theistic perspective. My general approach in each section will be to introduce a central philosophical question about happiness, lay out some of the leading positions and theories found in the historical and contemporary literature, and explain the implications of theism for answering the question and evaluating the positions and theories. I will not try to answer the "big questions" about happiness pure and simple, defend a particular theory of happiness, or consider all the arguments for and against the competing views. That is a different project for a different work. Instead, my analysis and argument will be conditional in nature: If God exists, how should we answer these questions and evaluate these positions and theories? If we assume a theistic perspective, what does it mean for human happiness?

This inquiry falls under various fields of philosophy, including moral philosophy, philosophy of religion, and a new subfield known as "the axiology of theism," which addresses questions that have mostly been overlooked in contemporary philosophy. There are three major types of philosophical questions about theism: (1) metaphysical questions about God's existence and nature,

God's relationship to creation, and so on; (2) epistemological questions about the knowledge of God, the rationality of belief in God, and so on; and (3) axiological questions about whether God's existence or non-existence is (or would be) a good thing or a bad thing. This Element addresses questions of the third kind.

Since the axiology of theism is a newer field that investigates unfamiliar topics, it is worth saying a bit more about it. Klaas Kraay, one of the leading philosophers in this area, introduces it this way: "Here is a provocative question: does it *matter* whether God exists? ... What *axiological difference* would – or does – theism make? ... [what is] the axiological import of God's existence, nature, and activity if theism is true, and, conversely, the axiological import of God's *non*existence, if theism is false[?]" (2021: 1). This inquiry can be broken up into various sub-questions depending on what *kind of value* we are considering (e.g., prudential goodness, goodness simpliciter, moral goodness, cosmic justice, suffering, autonomy, privacy) and what the *value-bearer* is (e.g., worlds, the lives of persons, persons themselves, non-human creatures). The two most popular positions are called "pro-theism" and "anti-theism." *Pro-theism* is the view that God's existence is (or would be) a good thing. *Anti-theism* is the view that God's existence is (or would be) a bad thing.[2]

The project of this Element can be situated within the axiology of theism. I will focus on one kind of value – happiness – and I will defend a pro-theism position concerning both the goodness of individual human lives and the goodness of the actual world. The question can be put like this: With respect to human happiness, is it better or worse if God exists? The answer I will give is that it is better for us and a better world if God exists. For the reasons mentioned earlier concerning the relevance of happiness to the evaluation of worldviews, this pro-theism answer is a good reason to give theism serious consideration (or reconsideration).

1.4 God

This Element is titled *God and Happiness*, so it is crucial to define these two key terms. We have already defined "happiness," but we have not yet clarified the meaning of "God" and "theism," which is necessary because the word "God" and the position known as "theism" are not monolithic. In this Element, *theism* refers to the metaphysical doctrine that God exists, not the epistemological notion of belief in God. *Atheism* refers to the view that God does not exist. I will

---

[2] I follow Kraay's (2021: 2) formulation of these two positions with slight modifications of my own. Kraay identifies three additional positions: (1) neutralism: things are neither better nor worse on theism than on atheism; (2) agnosticism: we should suspend judgment on the question; (3) quietism: the question is unanswerable in principle. I ignore these other options and limit my focus to pro-theism and anti-theism.

operate with a classical understanding of God that is widely shared among theistic philosophical traditions and the monotheistic religious traditions of Judaism, Christianity, and Islam (see Peterson *et al.* 2013: Ch. 7; Davies 2021: Ch. 1). However, I will draw primarily on the Christian intellectual tradition to articulate the theistic perspective, and my default version of theism will be Christian monotheism, for two reasons. The first is that it is one of the oldest and richest traditions of philosophical and theological reflection on happiness, it is the dominant form of theism in the history of Western philosophy and in contemporary philosophy, and most of the literature engages with Christian theism. The second is that it is the tradition I belong to and know best.

Central to the classical concept of God are the propositions that God is the *creator and first cause*, and that God is the *greatest conceivable being*. The first idea gives rise to a method in philosophical theology that centers on God as *absolutely metaphysically ultimate*: the most fundamental reality, the source of all reality other than God, the primary cause of all existing things, and the ultimate explanation of everything, including phenomena such as existence, contingent being, and change (see Aquinas 1920). This way of thinking about God entails that he is an infinite, immaterial, necessary, self-existent, simple, eternal, omnipresent, and supernatural being who created everything and transcends our spatiotemporal universe. The second idea gives rise to the method of perfect being theology, where God is construed as an *absolutely perfect being* who is supremely excellent and worthy of worship, and attributes of God are derived from reflection on what such a being must be like (see Anselm 2007c). This way of understanding God entails that he possesses essential attributes such as omniscience, omnipotence, perfect goodness, beauty, and other perfections. It also entails that God is in some way identical to truth, goodness, and beauty themselves; God is the source, locus, and paradigmatic exemplar of all truth, goodness, and beauty.

God is also a *personal* being. God is not an abstract object like a Platonic Form, a law of nature like Newton's laws of motion, or an impersonal cosmic energy like the Force. Instead, he is a person in the classical sense of a being who possesses intellect and will (or, in the standard Boethian formula, an "individual substance of a rational nature"). God has knowledge, freedom, and the ability to enter into relationships with other persons.[3]

---

[3] Not all theists agree with all of the preceding claims about God's nature and attributes. There is a debate among contemporary philosophers and theologians between two views that are sometimes labeled "classical theism" and "theistic personalism," and much of it centers on how terms should be predicated of God, how divine simplicity should be understood, and whether or not God is "a person." The way in which I am identifying God with truth, goodness, and beauty, and the sense in which I am describing God as a person (or, if one prefers, as "personal"), are not intended to assume any position in this debate and are being used in a generic sense that both camps should accept. For further study, see Peterson *et al.* (2013: Ch. 7); Davies (2021: Ch. 1).

There are three divine attributes that have special relevance to the topics explored in this Element and merit further elaboration. The first is God's status as *creator*. God is the creating and sustaining cause of all things other than himself. God made human beings as part of his providential plan for the universe, and he designed them with a certain nature: a common and essential human nature that all human beings share and that makes them all human (as opposed to a different kind of being). The second divine attribute is *intelligence*. God is supremely knowledgeable, rational, and wise. His activity, including his creation of human beings and human nature, is rational and intentional activity done for a purpose. God's "eternal law" or wise plan for the universe governs all things, including human beings, and orders them to the ends for which God created them. The third divine attribute is *goodness*. God's perfect goodness encompasses every kind of goodness there is, including intrinsic goodness simpliciter or excellence, metaphysical goodness or fullness of being, aesthetic goodness or beauty, epistemic goodness or truth, moral goodness or virtue, and personal goodness or dignity (see Stump and Kretzmann 1988; Adams 1999; Garcia 2008).[4] God's moral goodness includes (but is not limited to) his being *all-loving*. In the Christian tradition, God's love is usually understood as *agape* or charity: unconditional, other-directed, self-giving love. Following Aquinas, this kind of love can be defined as willing the good of the other and willing union with the other (Aquinas 1920: II-II, q. 23–26; Stump 2010: Ch. 5). God loves all human persons in the sense that he desires the good of all persons and union with all persons.

This is a brief and incomplete sketch of the traditional understanding of God's nature and attributes, but it is enough to give us a working concept of God that will be assumed throughout the volume. It also lets us make our first connection between God and happiness. Theism implies that God created us to be happy and wills our happiness. This section began with the claim that every human being wants to be happy, and that claim was rooted in human nature. Now we are adding that God wants every human being to be happy; and this claim is rooted in the divine nature.

One way to arrive at this conclusion is to show that it follows from God's status as our benevolent creator. On the theistic perspective, happiness is one of God's purposes in creating human beings. The first line of the *Catechism of the Catholic Church* reads: "God, infinitely perfect and blessed in himself, in a plan of sheer goodness freely created man to make him share in his own blessed life" (1995: Para. 1). And the beginning of the *Westminster Shorter Catechism* asks,

---

[4] Another sort of goodness that is sometimes attributed to God is happiness: the notion that God is perfectly happy, or, stronger, that God is happiness itself. For an exposition and defense of the classical position that God has the attribute of being all happy, see Stenberg (2019).

"What is the chief end of man? Answer: Man's chief end is to glorify God, and to enjoy him forever" (1647). Even if we could not know that happiness is one of God's purposes in creating us, the conclusion that God wills our happiness can be derived from God's goodness. Because he is all good and all loving, he wills our good in every respect, and happiness is a crucial aspect of the human good. God desires that every created person have a good life, and happiness is an essential part of the good life. A parent analogy is applicable here, given that many theists conceive of God as a father. All good parents want their children to be happy. If they did not, we would rightly judge them to be bad parents. So, if God can be understood as a loving father and every human person can be understood as one of his children, God must want everyone to be happy.[5]

Two objections might be lodged against this claim. The first is that some versions of theism maintain (explicitly or implicitly) that God does *not* want all human persons to be happy and instead positively wills for some to be unhappy. In my view, any such theology has a defective conception of God and cannot truly affirm that God is perfectly good and loving. An adequate understanding of God must include the idea that God wills the happiness of every created person.

The second objection is the problem of evil. It might seem that the propositions *God wants everyone to be happy* and *God is omnipotent, omniscient, and perfectly good* are logically inconsistent with, or improbable in light of, the unhappiness we observe in the world. The problem of suffering is a separate and enormous topic that cannot be dealt with in this work. But this objection, like the first one, prompts an important clarification. My claim about God's desire for human happiness pertains to what God wills *simpliciter* but not necessarily *secundum quid*, God's "antecedent" or "absolute" will as opposed to God's "consequent" or "permissive" will. Roughly, the distinction is between what God unqualifiedly would will if everything were up to him alone and worked out for the best, versus what God willingly permits in light of the free choices of creatures, which could be only the best thing available in the circumstances (see Stump 2010: Ch. 13–14). I am not claiming that if God exists then everyone *actually will be* happy. Human unhappiness is compatible with God's existence, and there are good reasons why God might allow some individuals to be unhappy despite his desire for their happiness.

God's desire for universal human happiness is one significant implication of theism. But we have not yet seen what happiness really is, what the elements of

---

[5] See Goetz (2012) for a defense of the stronger position that on a theistic perspective happiness is *the sole* purpose of life. See Walls (2002: Ch. 1–3) for another argument that God desires the happiness of every human person, which has some similarities to the one offered here.

a happy life are, and whether it is possible for anyone to be happy. These questions will be explored in the next three sections.

2 The Nature of Happiness

This section addresses the question, "What is happiness?" We have defined *happiness* as a life that is good for a person and goes well for the one living it, in the sense that pertains to an individual's well-being or flourishing. But this only tells us what concept we are investigating; it does not tell us what happiness itself really is. The "What is it?" question that asks for the nature or essential properties of a thing is one of the main sorts of question that philosophers ask, going all the way back to Socrates. As far as happiness is concerned, the importance of the question stems from the plausible assumption that having a correct understanding of the nature of happiness will be both theoretically and practically valuable. We cannot understand happiness unless we know what it is, and if we know what it is then we will be more likely to attain it because we will know what goal to aim at.

2.1 The Nature of Happiness: Two Questions

A helpful place to start an inquiry into the nature of happiness is the question, "Is happiness subjective or objective?" This form of the question is ambiguous, and there are two different ways of interpreting it based on two different senses of subjectivity and objectivity. One is the *metaethical question* about the status of propositions or truths about happiness. Are there objective truths about happiness that are universally true for all human beings independently of what anyone believes or practices? Or do happiness claims have a subjective truth-value that is determined by human individuals or groups in some way? The alternative interpretation is the *normative question* about the nature of happiness itself. What are the good-making features of a life that explain why someone is happy? Are they subjective sorts of things – mental states or experiences – or are they objective in nature – things other than subjective mental states or experiences? We will consider the implications of theism for both of these questions.

2.2 Theism and the Metaethical Question

The metaethical question is whether happiness propositions have a subjective truth-value or an objective truth-value. Take the proposition *Mary is happy*. The typical subjectivist answer is that the metaethical truth-maker for this proposition is some subjective feature of Mary, such as her belief or judgment about whether she is happy. On this view, happiness is relative to individuals, and it is impossible or rare for us to be mistaken about our own happiness. Mary is the infallible and authoritative judge of her own happiness, and her life is going well for her if she believes it is. The objectivist answer is that the metaethical truth-maker for *Mary is happy* is an objective fact that is independent of Mary's (and anyone else's) beliefs, judgments, practices, and so on. On this view, happiness is universal, and there is an objectively correct way to evaluate how well a person's life is going. Mary (like the rest of us) is not an infallible judge of her own happiness and can be mistaken about it.

Theism implies that happiness is objective in the metaethical sense. Propositions about happiness have an objective truth-value that is independent of us; there are universal facts about human happiness that we discover rather than invent; and we can be wrong about what happiness is and whether we are truly happy. One way to arrive at this conclusion is to infer it from God's attributes and activities. As I argued in Section 1, the theistic perspective holds that one of God's purposes in creating human beings is our happiness. God, being all good, designed human nature in such a way that happiness is (at least) one of our primary ends in life. And, being all loving, God wills that everyone experience happiness as one component of his or her overall good. On this way of looking at it, the metaethical truth-makers for propositions about human happiness are objective facts about God's nature and will, God's design of human nature, and God's purposes for human life.

This answer to the metaethical question provides a strong ontological grounding for objective facts about happiness and a good explanation of them. Theism's robust metaethical foundation is superior to an alternative non-theistic approach that might, for example, consider objective truths about happiness to be brute facts with no deeper metaphysical grounding or explanation. On theism, truths about happiness are anchored in the most ultimate reality and explanation there is: God.

2.3 The Normative Question

Recall that the normative version of the question "What is happiness?" asks about the nature of happiness itself. What makes a person or a life happy? Suppose we are wondering whether it will be beneficial to start exercising regularly, spend more time reading, learn to play an instrument, change jobs, or get married. For each of these things, we can ask whether it *really is* good for us, and if so, what *explains* its goodness. Philosophical theories of happiness aim to answer these questions and say what is good and why. Theories of the *nature* of happiness explain why things are good by identifying the ultimate good-making features of lives, the normative properties that explain the truth of propositions like "*G* is good for *S*" (where *S* stands for an individual subject and

G stands for a good thing, activity, or state of affairs). Theories of the *content* of happiness identify the specific goods that possess the good-making properties, the things can be substituted for *G* in true sentences of the form "*G* is good for *S*" (see Murphy 2001: 46–48). Sometimes this distinction is put in terms of "explanatory theories" versus "enumerative theories" (see Crisp 2006: 102–103). Something can contribute to happiness as part of its nature, or its content, or both. This section focuses on the nature of happiness, and the next section focuses on the content of happiness.

Philosophical theories are primarily about the nature of happiness, and they are after what is *intrinsically*, *fundamentally*, and *directly* good for a person: something that is good in itself as an end rather than a means, is a basic good, and provides an immediate benefit. The contrast is with goods that are instrumental, derivative, and indirect.[6] Consider something that can be good for a person: playing a game of basketball. The reason why it can be good is that it realizes or brings about something distinct from basketball that gives it its value, perhaps pleasure, satisfaction, health, friendship, achievement, or athletic excellence. Playing basketball is instrumentally, derivatively, and indirectly good for the player in virtue of its relation to one of these other goods, which are the real candidates for basic intrinsic goods.

Theories of happiness are primarily theories of what is intrinsically prudentially valuable or intrinsically good for a person.[7] In developing these theories, philosophers try to identify the ultimate good-making features or properties that explain why a person or a life is happy. I will call them the *good-makers*. The normative question about the nature of happiness is about the nature of the good-makers. The general question is whether they are subjective or objective phenomena, and the specific question is exactly which phenomena they are.

There are two general and formal positions on the nature of happiness. They differ on whether an individual's mental state or pro-attitude is what makes something good for the individual (where "mental state" and "pro-attitude" usually refer to pleasure or desire). *Subjectivism* holds that a good *G* is good for a subject *S* solely in virtue of *S*'s mental states or attitudes toward *G*, most commonly because *G* gives *S* pleasure or satisfies one of *S*'s desires.[8]

---

[6] I often will use "intrinsically valuable" as shorthand for "intrinsically, fundamentally, and directly valuable."

[7] These theories also speak to what is bad and harmful for persons, but for the sake of simplicity my discussion will leave badness aside. Accounts of unhappiness are usually the mirror opposite of accounts of happiness and logically dependent on them. For example, if happiness consists in desire satisfaction, then unhappiness consists in desire frustration.

[8] Pleasure and desire are not the only subjective features that a subjective theory of happiness might use. Another candidate for the subjective good-maker is the subject's personal "values," where happiness is analyzed in terms of value fulfillment. I leave aside such theories here, limiting the discussion to pleasure and desire, which are the most popular forms of subjectivism.

Objectivism holds that what is good for someone is not a function of subjective mental states or attitudes, but is a matter of attaining objective goods. A good G is good for S whether or not S has any mental state or attitude toward G, such as enjoying G or desiring G. The dispute between these two positions concerns attitude-dependence. Subjectivists maintain that the goodness of something depends on the subjective pro-attitudes of the subject in question. For example, they would say that playing basketball is good for a person – let's call him Chris – *if and only if*, and *because*, Chris enjoys basketball or wants to play basketball (or because he enjoys or wants something it brings). Objectivists deny attitude-dependence and maintain that goodness is independent of the subject's pro-attitudes. They would say that playing basketball can be good for Chris even if he does not enjoy it or desire it, in virtue of the fact that it realizes some objective good, such as health, achievement, or friendship (for further study, see Fletcher 2016; Heathwood 2021).[9]

Falling within these two general camps are various specific and substantive theories of happiness. I will focus on the five leading theories.[10] The first one is *hedonism*, which says that what is intrinsically good for a person is experiences of pleasure (aka enjoyment). Everything else has only instrumental value insofar as it brings pleasure. Our level of happiness is determined by the overall amount of pleasure we experience in life.

Variants of hedonism can be differentiated according to their views of what pleasure is and what kinds of pleasure count. Two of the most influential hedonists, Jeremy Bentham and John Stuart Mill, disagree on these points. Bentham's *quantitative hedonism* recognizes only bodily pleasures and holds that only the quantity of pleasure matters. According to Mill's *qualitative hedonism*, there are two types of pleasure: lower-order bodily pleasures such as eating, drinking, sex, and rest; and higher-order mental pleasures such as friendship, knowledge, art, and virtue. For Mill, happiness is determined by both the quantity and the quality of pleasure, with mental pleasures being

---

[9] The dispute about normative subjectivism/objectivism covered in this subsection should not be conflated with the dispute about metaethical subjectivism/objectivism covered in the previous subsection. Both of the specific theories mentioned in this Element that are classified as normatively subjectivist (hedonism and desire satisfactionism) can be coupled with metaethical objectivism. They can hold that happiness propositions have objective truth-values and there are objectively correct answers about whether people are happy, and the correct answers (when fully analyzed) will identify subjective attitudes as the thing that makes people happy. These theories can maintain that individuals are not infallible and authoritative judges of their own happiness and could be mistaken about it (for example, they might not know what they really desire).

[10] In addition to the five theories covered in this Element, there are also hybrid theories and pluralistic theories that combine two or more of them. They will not be explored in this Element, but a few will be mentioned later in this section.

intrinsically qualitatively better and contributing more to a person's happiness. Another distinction we can make is between sensory pleasure and attitudinal pleasure, where the former is a bodily sensation (such as the delicious taste of ice cream), and the latter is a mental attitude of taking pleasure in something (such as the enjoyment of watching children play) (for contemporary defenses, see Feldman 2004; Crisp 2006).

According to the second theory, *desire satisfactionism*, what is intrinsically good for a person is the satisfaction of his or her desires (or preferences): when an individual desires X and X occurs; when something is the way one wants it to be. Everything else has only instrumental value insofar as it gets us what we want. We have stronger and weaker desires, and we want some things more than others. The stronger the desire, the better it is for us to satisfy. Because we can have conflicting desires, our level of happiness is determined by the net balance of our strongest desires; what is best for us is to get what we want most. Thomas Hobbes and Immanuel Kant (on one reading) are two famous historical proponents of this theory (for contemporary defenses, see Sobel 2016; Heathwood 2021).

The two main varieties of desire satisfactionism differ on which desires matter. According to *actual desire theory*, what is good for a person is the satisfaction of the desires she actually has. According to *ideal desire theory*, what is good for a person is the satisfaction of the desires she would have if she were sufficiently informed and rational, which could be different from her actual desires. The first theory looks to the desires of the real person, whereas the second looks to the desires of a hypothetical, counterfactual version of that person. The two approaches often have the same implications when it comes to what is good, but sometimes they diverge. To see how this can happen, consider the character George Bailey from the classic film *It's a Wonderful Life*. When George is at his most despondent as a result of long-term frustration and disappointment and the threat of financial ruin and public scandal, he considers suicide. His plan to jump off a wintry bridge is foiled by the intervention of the angel Clarence. But this does not change George's attitude; he soon tells Clarence that he wishes he had never been born. Assuming that this reflects his strongest desires, a simple version of actual desire theory implies that what is good for George is death or non-existence. But as the rest of the film shows, this is not the only way to look at it. George glimpses an alternate reality in which he never existed, where he comes to see that his town and his loved ones are worse off without him. After his depressing and enlightening experience there, he proclaims that he wants to live again. By the end of the film, the viewer is meant to agree with George that he has a wonderful life. We can understand George's transformation through the lens of ideal desire theory. When he becomes better informed as a result of living in a world with no George Bailey in it, and when he is thinking more rationally and no longer in the grip of emotion, he wants to live. The desires that are good to satisfy are the desires of "ideal George" in his final state, not the desires of "actual George" prior to his transformation.

Hedonism and desire satisfactionism are both subjective theories of happiness because their respective good-makers – pleasure and desire – are subjective phenomena, that is, psychological experiences, mental states, or pro-attitudes. The next group of theories are objective ones that recognize good-makers that are independent of a subject's attitudes.

Objective list theory, the third on our list, says that what is intrinsically good for someone is attaining objective goods. There are multiple objective goods that can be put on a list, and all the items on the list are distinct and irreducible basic goods. The more of these goods a person realizes in her life, and the higher the degree of their realization, the happier she will be. This is the newest of the five theories of happiness, and some of its earliest proponents are the twentieth-century philosophers W.D. Ross and Derek Parfit (for contemporary defenses, see Rice 2013; Hooker 2015).[11]

Varieties of objective list theory are differentiated according to the items on their lists. Some widely recognized objective goods include friendship, knowledge, achievement, autonomy, beauty, pleasure, and virtue. Because objective list theory is pluralistic, maintaining that there is more than one intrinsic good, another way that versions of it can differ is how they see the relationship between the goods on the list. They could be incomparable in value, equally valuable, more or less valuable, hierarchically ordered, and so on. In addition to pluralism about intrinsic goods, another key feature of objective list theory is that there is no deeper unifying explanation for what makes all of the items on the list good; they are all fundamental goods in their own right. The furthest we can go is to say that something is good for a person because it instantiates one or more of the objective goods.

The fourth theory is *perfectionism*, another objective theory which says that what is intrinsically good for a person is the perfection or fulfillment of his human nature. On this view, all human beings share a common human nature that endows them with characteristic human capacities or powers. Human flourishing consists in the development and exercise of these capacities, such as the physical, intellectual, volitional, social, and emotional powers; and the realization of their corresponding ends, such as life and health, knowledge, free agency, friendship, and beauty. Our level of happiness is determined by the

---

[11] Ross and Thomas Hurka (mentioned later) present their views as accounts of goodness simpliciter as opposed to goodness-for, but they can also be formulated as theories of happiness/well-being.

degree to which we fulfill these capacities and participate in these goods. Aristotle and Thomas Aquinas are two prominent defenders of perfectionism (for contemporary defenses, see Hurka 1993; Kraut 2007).

Different versions of the theory operate with different conceptions of human nature and of the capacities that matter for human flourishing. Three mainstream approaches hold that the relevant capacities are ones that are *unique* to human beings (i.e., possessed by humans and no other creatures), ones that are *fundamental* to human activity (i.e., involved in virtually all human activities), and ones that humans possess *essentially* (capacities that make up the essence of the human substance, or necessary properties that humans possess in every possible world). Many perfectionists affirm the traditional Aristotelian position that to be human is to be a *rational animal*: the capacities constitutive of rationality and animality are the essential human powers that make us the kind of being we are. And many of them think that certain human capacities are more important than others, especially the rational powers of intellect and will, which are fulfilled by goods such as knowledge, freedom, and friendship.

The fifth and final theory, *eudaimonism*, says that what is intrinsically good for us is virtuous activity.[12] Happiness is a matter of cultivating and exercising the virtues, including moral virtues like justice, courage, and temperance, and intellectual virtues like practical wisdom, curiosity, and intellectual honesty. Our level of happiness is determined by how virtuous we are in our character and behavior. Virtue primarily (but not exclusively) involves moral goodness. What is good for someone is having excellent moral character; possessing habits of acting, thinking, feeling, and desiring in morally appropriate ways; doing the right thing; and acting in accordance with moral laws, principles, obligations, and rights. This approach has a long history in philosophy, and its defenders include the Greeks Plato and Aristotle, the Stoics Seneca and Cicero, and the Confucians Mencius and Xunzi (for contemporary defenses, see Annas 1993; Russell 2012). More than any of the other theories, eudaimonism denies a hard separation between happiness and morality by making them at least partly overlap.

There are different ways that virtue might be related to happiness, not all of which are definitive of eudaimonism. For example, virtue might be a necessary condition for happiness, a sufficient condition for happiness, or the most reliable way to achieve happiness (for further study, see Baril 2016). Eudaimonism in general affirms that virtue is *intrinsically* beneficial, *necessary* for happiness, and at least *partially constitutive* of happiness. Some versions make the stronger

---

[12] I am using the term "eudaimonism" to refer only to a theory of happiness, not a theory of practical reasoning, motivation, or an overall good life.

claim that virtue is necessary *and sufficient* for happiness, or that happiness consists in *virtue alone*; but these are not essential tenets of eudaimonism as such. The most famous eudaimonist in the history of philosophy is Aristotle, and most contemporary versions of the theory are modeled on his account. On an Aristotelian view, the happy life involves the cultivation and active exercise of the moral and intellectual virtues. Happiness consists essentially and primarily (but not wholly) in virtuous activity, and virtue is necessary (but not sufficient) for happiness. Happiness also requires a long and complete life, as well as sufficient "external goods" – friends, good fortune, resources like wealth and power, and the proper upbringing and moral education (Aristotle 1984: Bk. 1).

To see how these five theories explain the nature of happiness differently, consider the following example. Dan sets out to throw a party, in fact, the biggest and best party his social group has ever seen (or at least the closest thing to a Great Gatsby party he and his friends can afford on their modest budget). The event is a huge success, with a record turnout and a good time had by all. All five theories of happiness can say that hosting the party is good for Dan, but they will give different explanations as to why. Hedonism says that it is good for Dan because hosting and socializing with friends brings him pleasure. Desire satisfactionism says that it is good because Dan wants to have an epic party and that is what happens. According to objective list theory, the activity is good for Dan because it realizes the objective goods of friendship and achievement. According to perfectionism, its goodness lies in the fact that it involves the exercise of Dan's intellectual and social capacities and fulfills these aspects of his nature (it has been said that man is by nature a rational animal and a party animal). The eudaimonist answer is that hosting the party increases Dan's happiness because it manifests virtues such as generosity, friendliness, and hospitality.

In addition to providing different specific accounts of the good-makers, these five theories fall into separate camps on the more general issue of subjectivism versus objectivism. For hedonism and desire theory, the good-maker is a subjective phenomenon. What confers intrinsic value on Dan's activity is a subjective experience or mental state of his – pleasure or desire. For the other three theories, the good-maker is an objective feature of Dan's activity. What confers value on it is the fact that it instantiates brute objective goods, nature-fulfillment, or virtue.

2.4 Theism and the Normative Question

The rest of this section will explore connections between theism and the theories covered in the previous subsection. The two questions we will address are: (1) Whether theism implies that one of the two general positions on the nature of happiness – subjectivism or objectivism – is the correct one, and (2) Whether theism implies that one (or more) of the five specific theories of the nature of happiness is correct. My answer to both questions will be the kind of answer one often hears from philosophers: "No and yes, in different respects."

Theism does not logically entail that either of the two general positions or any of the five specific theories is correct. From the assumption of theism, nothing necessarily follows about the nature of happiness. Theists have defended different theories of happiness, and there is no consensus among contemporary theistic philosophers on the issue. In fact, there are prominent contemporary theistic proponents of every theory we have seen. For example, Stuart Goetz (2012) defends hedonism, Thomas Carson (2000) defends desire satisfactionism, Hud Hudson (2021) defends objective list theory, Mark Murphy (2001) defends perfectionism, and David McPherson (2020) defends eudaimonism. Theists also defend hybrid views with elements of multiple theories. For instance, Robert Adams's (1999) account is a combination of hedonism and objective list theory, and William Lauinger's (2012) is a combination of desire satisfactionism and perfectionism. One advantage of theism is that it is compatible with all the leading theories of happiness, making them all live options. For a theist who is a convinced proponent of one of these theories, there will be no logical inconsistency among her views, and there will be a way to harmonize her beliefs about theism and happiness. Whatever the right answer is about the nature of happiness, it fits with theism.

Another significant advantage of theism is that it can accommodate and validate the central idea behind all five theories of happiness: pleasure, desire, objective goods, nature fulfillment, and virtue. Boethius says that "happiness is a state brought about by the convergence of all good things" (2001: Bk. III, Prose 2), and all good things are found in God. Following Boethius, Thomas Aquinas says that in the happiness that comes from union with God, "there will be the aggregate of all good things, because whatever good there be in these things, we shall possess it all in the Supreme Fount of goodness" (1920: I-II, q. 4, a. 7). He argues that "all other beatitude is included in the beatitude of God" (1920: I, q. 26, a. 4), and "the perfection of the divine blessedness can be observed from the fact that it includes within itself every blessedness in a most perfect way" (1955: I, Ch. 102). Aquinas explains:

> Whatever is desirable in whatsoever beatitude, whether true or false, pre-exists wholly and in a more eminent degree in the divine beatitude. As to contemplative happiness, God possesses a continual and most certain contemplation of himself and of all things else; and as to that which is active, he has the governance of the whole universe. As to earthly happiness, which consists in pleasure, riches, power, honor, and fame, according to Boethius, he possesses joy in himself and all things else for his pleasure; instead of

> riches he has that complete self-sufficiency, which is promised by riches; in
> place of power, he has omnipotence; for honor, the government of all things;
> and in place of fame, he possesses the admiration of all creatures. (1920: I,
> q. 26, a. 4, slightly modified)

John Calvin expresses the point this way:

> If God contains in himself as an inexhaustible fountain all fullness of blessing,
> those who aspire to the supreme good and perfect happiness must not long for
> anything beyond him . . . If our Lord will share his glory, power, and righteous-
> ness, with the elect, nay, will give himself to be enjoyed by them – and what is
> better still, will, in a manner, become one with them – let us remember that
> every kind of happiness is herein included. (1845: Bk. III, Ch. 25)

The notion that all human happiness is a participation in God's happiness can be
understood as the idea that God is the archetype of all earthly goods. God
possesses all goods in a preeminent and supreme way, and all the things that
make for a happy life are found in God in a pure and perfect form. As Aquinas
puts it: "When we say, 'God is good,' . . . the meaning is, 'Whatever good we
attribute to creatures, pre-exists in God,' and in a more excellent and higher
way" (1920: I, q. 13, a. 2).

Boethius, Aquinas, and Calvin do not explicitly say how the divine goodness
contains all the types of goodness that define the five leading contemporary
theories of happiness, but we can supply such an explanation. When a human
person experiences union with God in the afterlife (i.e., in the heavenly state), it
will be the most pleasant experience possible, for every source of pleasure (with
the exception of inherently evil pleasures) will be found in God, the source of all
good things. With respect to desire, being in communion with the perfect and
infinite good that is God will satisfy all the desires of the human heart, for every
good thing we might desire can be found in God. Heavenly union with God will
also involve participation in every objective good, for example, everlasting life
and unfailing health, untarnished friendship and social harmony with God and
other created persons, maximal knowledge and understanding through the human
mind's connection to the omniscient mind of God, and the aesthetic experience of
beholding the beauty of God and the sublime order and harmony of the universe.
The heavenly state will also involve the full perfection of human nature, where the
purpose of human life will be achieved, human functioning will be optimized, and
all the natural human capacities will be fulfilled by the attainment of their
corresponding ends in the divine nature. As for virtue, union with a perfectly
good God demands that a human person be morally perfect, in the sense that one's
actions and character are in full conformity with God's will. Thus, moral goodness
is a requirement and an effect of the happiness that consists in union with God.

Section 3 will contain a fuller explanation and defense of these claims by exploring the nature of union with God and showing why it is the highest form of happiness. For present purposes, the take-away is that the theistic doctrine that God is goodness itself – the first cause, final end, paradigm, and perfection of all goods – is the fundamental reason why theists throughout the ages have said that happiness is found in God, however the nature of happiness is understood. It is also the main reason why contemporary philosophers are free to defend theistic versions of all five theories of happiness. No matter which one is correct – hedonism, desire satisfactionism, objective list theory, perfectionism, or eudaimonism – there is a way to construct a theistic account where God is the summit of human happiness. Moreover, theism does not demand a commitment to just one of the five theories. It allows for a pluralistic approach that combines elements of them all, because pleasure, desire, objective goods, human perfection, and virtue all have their most valuable realization in God. A theist can adopt one of the five theories, or a hybrid or pluralistic theory that combines one or more of them. Regardless of how the account is formulated, theism allows for a principled and attractive combination of all five core ideas that intuitively seem to be part of happiness and necessary to include in some way. Theism lets us have it all in a theory of happiness.

2.5 God and the Objectivity of Happiness

In the previous subsection, I explained why theism is compatible with all the leading theories of happiness and does not necessarily entail that happiness is subjective or objective in nature. In this subsection, I will argue that although theism does not *logically entail* that normative subjectivism or objectivism is correct, the *most probable* or *most plausible* theistic account of happiness is an objective one (such as objective list theory, perfectionism, or eudaimonism), or a hybrid or pluralistic one with an objective component (such as hedonism + objective list theory or desire satisfactionism + perfectionism), rather than a purely subjective one (such as hedonism or desire satisfactionism).[13] Theism makes objective theories more plausible than subjective theories. I will offer two arguments for this position.

The first is a historical argument. The vast majority of thinkers in the Christian tradition have endorsed objectivism about happiness, and subjectivism is a small minority view (see White 2006; Irwin 2007; Lauinger 2016).[14] This descriptive fact alone does not directly tell us anything about the truth of

---

[13] In what follows, "objective theories" will include both purely objective theories and hybrid or pluralistic theories with an objective component, and "subjective theories" will refer to purely subjective theories.

[14] From what I can tell, the same is true of the theistic tradition more broadly, not just the Christian stream of it. But for the sake of being careful and modest, I will limit my claim to Christianity.

objectivism, of course. But the historical evidence does indicate something significant, and it can provide the material for an argument from authority or testimony. Within the Christian tradition, the majority of thinkers in general, and virtually all of the greatest minds in particular, have not only affirmed the position that happiness is objective, but have defended this position with numerous arguments; and they have held that an objective conception of happiness is the default option for theists. If one considers these thinkers and the Christian intellectual tradition to have some kind of epistemic authority and weight when it comes to forming one's beliefs, then the consensus and testimony found in the historical record will provide some (inductive or abductive) evidence in favor of an objective conception of happiness. This point holds even though the authority of the tradition is not infallible or beyond reasonable dissent, and even though the historical evidence is not conclusive.

The second argument is a philosophical one. On a theistic perspective, the most important element of happiness and the best thing possible for a human person is union with God. Union with God is the highest good and final end for all human beings. All theists accept (or should accept) this claim. The most plausible way to understand this position is that union with God is *objectively* good for us, independently of our mental states and attitudes and whether or not we take pleasure in it or desire it. Even if it is necessarily the case, due to facts about human psychology and the divine nature, that we actually *do* or ideally *would* enjoy and desire union with God, and that union with God *will* bring us maximal pleasure and satisfaction, union with God is not good for us *because* we enjoy it or want it. An individual's subjective mental state is not what *makes* it good. It is good because the individual attains or communes with the highest objective value: God himself. It involves an objective relation between a human person and God: being in relationship with God, having an interpersonal connection to God, being in a state of knowing and loving God. It is this relationship *itself*, rather than just the pleasurable experience or the satisfaction that accompanies it, that is intrinsically good for us. Regardless of whether it is further analyzed in terms of objective goods, nature fulfillment, or virtuous activity, its goodness will be objective. A related point is that union with God is an *objectively necessary condition* for perfect happiness. Even maximal pleasure or desire satisfaction, in the absence of union with God, will not make someone completely happy.

Here is another way to formulate the argument. Subjective theories of happiness maintain that all the good-makers are subjective states involving pleasure or desire. On theism, at least one thing is objectively and intrinsically good for all human beings regardless of what they enjoy or desire: the good of union with God, which is a real relation between a human person and a divine person, not merely a subjective state. Happiness has an objective dimension because it requires the right kind of objective relation between a human individual and something external to the individual that has objective value. The essence of happiness is not found in things (e.g., wealth, possessions), experiences (e.g., fun activities, life experiences), accomplishments (e.g., work, achievement), honors (e.g., social status, fame), impersonal knowledge (e.g., philosophical wisdom, scientific understanding), or anything inside ourselves (e.g., self-esteem, inner peace). Instead, happiness is primarily found in other persons. The essence of happiness is a personal connection to another, most importantly to God. Pascal puts it the following way:

> We are full of things that impel us outwards. Our instinct makes us feel that our happiness must be sought outside ourselves. Our passions drive us outwards, even without objects to excite them. External objects tempt us in themselves and entice us even when we do not think about them. Thus it is no good philosophers telling us: Withdraw into yourselves and there you will find your good. We do not believe them, and those who do believe them are the most empty and silly of all. (1995: No. 143)

> The Stoics say: "Withdraw into yourself, that is where you will find peace." And that is not true. Others say: "Go outside: look for happiness in some diversion." And that is not true: we may fall sick. Happiness is neither outside nor inside us: it is in God, both outside and inside us. (1995: No. 407)

Augustine makes the same point more succinctly when he says that "our hearts are restless till they rest in [God]" (2006: Bk. I, Ch. 1).

In my view, these considerations count against purely subjective theories of happiness and make objective theories more plausible for theists.[15] They also bring to the forefront the key theistic doctrine that *union with God* is the greatest good. It will be explored in detail in the next section.

3 The Content and Structure of Happiness

The last section addressed the question of what happiness *is*. This section will explore the question of what happiness *consists in* or *includes*. The former asks *why* things are good for us, and the latter asks *what* things are good for us. This section will cover two major topics. The first is the *content of happiness*: the

---

[15] There are some theists who would most likely reject this conclusion and deny that objectivism is more plausible than subjectivism. But theistic subjectivists (e.g., Carson 2000; Goetz 2012) typically do not make an opposing case of the *same kind* that I am making here: a "top-down" argument that theism makes subjectivism more plausible than objectivism. Instead, their usual strategy is the opposite "bottom-up" method that first defends a subjective theory of happiness on independent grounds and then links it to theism. For this reason, these theistic subjectivists do not really pose an objection or counterargument to the one I give here, and they do not speak to the question of what *theism itself* implies about the nature of happiness.

constituents or ingredients of happiness. What are the various goods that contribute to happiness as parts of a happy life? The second is the *structure of happiness*: how these goods are organized and prioritized in a life. Is there a hierarchy of goods, with some being more valuable than others? Is there a single "greatest good" that is the most important? Or are none of the goods more or less valuable than others?

3.1 The Content of Happiness

When investigating the content of happiness, we are aiming to identify the most basic, general, and distinct goods that are the constituents of happiness. A traditional list of candidates used by many ancient and medieval philosophers includes wealth, honor, fame, power, pleasure, bodily goods like health and beauty, and spiritual goods like virtue and knowledge (see Aquinas 1920: I-II, q. 2). In contemporary philosophy, some widely recognized ingredients of happiness include life and health, knowledge and rationality, freedom and autonomy, relationships and community, work and achievement, pleasure and play, beauty and aesthetic experience, virtue and moral goodness, personal development and self-actualization, meaning and purpose, and emotional fulfillment (see Fletcher 2016).[16]

All five theories of happiness covered in Section 2 can recognize these various goods as part of the content of happiness. Where the theories will differ is how they explain the type of goodness they possess (e.g., intrinsic or instrumental value, fundamental or derivative value), and what ultimately makes them good (e.g., pleasantness, desirability, brute objective goodness, perfectiveness, or virtuousness). Likewise, theists can hold that the content of happiness includes all or some of the items on these lists.

Theism does have more definite and significant implications when it comes to a particular candidate for a source of happiness: religion or "spirituality." Is this something that contributes to human well-being? Both philosophers and psychologists have offered reasons to answer in the affirmative. Some proponents of objective list theory and perfectionism argue that religion is a basic human good. For them, religion typically is understood along the lines of harmony with a transcendent, ultimate reality that is the source of cosmic order, meaning, and value, which can take a variety of forms in different religious traditions (see Murphy 2001; Finnis 2011). Some defenders of eudaimonism identify a spiritual dimension of human flourishing (see McPherson 2020). There is

---

[16] Intriguingly, these philosophical lists have a considerable amount of resonance with contemporary research in positive psychology: a branch of social psychology devoted to the scientific study of happiness and well-being. For helpful overviews of the scientific literature that illustrate the overlap, see Helliwell, Layard, and Sachs (2012: Ch. 3); Haybron (2013).

also a large amount of empirical data on religion and happiness. In psychological studies, religion or spirituality is frequently recognized as a source of happiness, and religious people tend to report higher happiness levels than non-religious people (Helliwell, Layard, and Sachs 2012: Ch. 2).[17] Philosophical reflection and empirical evidence, then, provide some initial grounds for thinking that religion is a human good.

However, the way we understand the meaning of "religion" matters and makes a difference. Rather than the thin and generic notion of religion or spirituality typically found in the philosophical and psychological literature, we need one that is more substantive and specific. I will understand the good of religion along the lines of *union with God*. We have seen in previous sections that union with God is central to the theistic view of happiness. Later in this section we will explore the nature of union with God in more detail, and we will consider reasons for thinking that it is not just one part of a happy life but the most important part.

3.2 The Structure of Happiness

To ask about the structure of happiness is to ask how all the various elements of happiness should be organized within a life, and whether there is any order of value among goods. Of course, different individuals can have conflicting *opinions* about the relative priority of goods and can choose their own *subjective* hierarchy. But that is neither controversial nor philosophically interesting. The important question is whether there is an *objective* hierarchy of goods that is independent of anyone's beliefs and choices.

We will begin once again by identifying some common opinions on the issue. Ancient and medieval philosophers engaged in a centuries-long debate about the *summum bonum* or highest good. Almost all of them agreed that there is one, but they disagreed about what it is. John Stuart Mill memorably writes:

> From the dawn of philosophy, the question concerning the *summum bonum*, or, what is the same thing, concerning the foundation of morality, has been accounted the main problem in speculative thought, has occupied the most gifted intellects and divided them into sects and schools .... And after more than two thousand years the same discussions continue ... and neither thinkers nor mankind at large seem nearer to being unanimous on the subject, than when the youth Socrates listened to the old Protagoras. (2001: 1)

The same traditional list of the sources of happiness that we saw earlier also gives us the usual suspects for the greatest good: wealth, honor, fame, power,

---

[17] See Kaczor (2019) for a detailed study of the ways in which positive psychology supports the claim that religion is a contributor to happiness and confirms many of the central beliefs and practices of Christianity regarding what happiness involves and how it can be achieved.

pleasure, bodily goods like health and beauty, and spiritual goods like virtue and knowledge. For example, Epicureans maintained that it was pleasure, while Platonists, Aristotelians, Stoics, and Confucians held that it was virtue.

When it comes to contemporary philosophers, the consensus is much different, with most thinkers denying an objective scale of value and dismissing the idea of a *summum bonum*. Proponents of subjective theories like hedonism and desire satisfactionism reject an objective and universal hierarchy because in their view prudential goodness is subjective in nature, and pleasure and desire are person-relative: the hierarchy of value (if one exists) will depend on the idiosyncratic pleasures or desires of the individual in question. Objective list theorists typically hold that all the basic objective goods are in themselves either equally valuable or incomparable, and it is a matter of subjective preference or autonomous choice how individuals order the goods within their own life plans. Many perfectionists take a similar position (see, for example, Murphy 2001; Kraut 2007; Finnis 2011). But some affirm a hierarchy of value, with the dominant view placing intellectual goods at the top (see, for example, Hurka 1993). Eudaimonists are the outlier because they typically hold that virtue is the supreme good. They offer different hierarchies of the virtues, however, with some arguing that the most important one is practical wisdom, others that it is charity, and others that it is empathy.

In contrast to the mainstream position in contemporary philosophy that denies an objective hierarchy of goods, theism implies such a hierarchy. On the theistic perspective, there is one good that is more valuable and more important for human happiness than all the others. This good is union with God, which is considered the *summum bonum*, greatest good, and final end of human beings. The theistic tradition has held that union with God is the *unum necessarium*: the "one thing necessary" for true happiness. In addition to being the most valuable good, it is also the central good around which others are organized; it structures and orders the other goods.

We have already encountered this idea in previous sections, and it has been endorsed by virtually every theistic philosopher who has spoken to the question of happiness. Calvin, for instance, says that "it is the very summit of happiness to enjoy the presence of God" (1845: Bk. III, Ch. 9). According to Augustine,

> [God] is the source of our happiness, and he is the end of all desire. In electing him . . . we set our course toward him in love, so that, when we reach him, we may be at rest, blessed because made perfect by the one who is our ultimate end. For our good, the final good about which there is so much dispute among the philosophers, is nothing other than to cling to him by whose incorporeal embrace alone, if one can speak of such a thing, the intellectual soul is filled and made fertile with true virtues. (2012: Bk. III, Ch. 3)

Boethius identifies happiness itself with God: "God is highest and is most full of the Good that is highest and perfect; but we have established that true happiness is the highest Good; therefore, it is necessary that true happiness is located in this highest God" (2001: Bk. III, Prose 10).

The thesis that union with God is the supreme good raises two important questions that call for deeper reflection: (1) *What* exactly is union with God? (2) *Why* is union with God the greatest good? We will consider these questions in order.

3.3 The Nature of Union with God

If union with God is the best thing possible for a human being, it is plausible to suppose that it must somehow involve the whole human person and complete human well-being in all its dimensions, encompassing every aspect of human nature and every human good. That being said, within the theistic tradition there is wide agreement on the general meaning of union with God as essentially and centrally a matter of *knowing and loving God*. Aquinas speaks on behalf of the tradition when he remarks that "God is the last end of man and of all other things ... [and] man and other rational creatures attain to their last end by knowing and loving God" (1920: I-II, q. 1, a. 8). On this view, the activity or state of union with God is primarily a function of the rational and personal human capacities of intellect and will, whose corresponding ends and activities are, respectively, knowing and loving, or truth and love. The heart of true happiness is knowing and loving God, which represents the maximal fulfillment of the powers of intellect and will and the goods of intellectual understanding and loving relationship. All the other goods flow from it.

There is consensus in the theistic tradition that union with God in general consists in knowing and loving God. But when we try to understand its meaning more deeply and specifically, we encounter diverging views. Theists disagree about where the emphasis should be and which one – knowing or loving, intellect or will – is metaphysically and axiologically primary, which is prior in the order of being and higher in the order of value. The two major positions in this debate are the *intellectual model* and the *social model*. According to the former, union with God is construed in terms of *knowledge*, as an act of the intellect understanding God as *truth*. It is an intellectual union consisting of speculative knowledge of God, which is primarily a contemplative activity of the intellect in its capacity to know. On the alternative social model, union with God is understood in terms of *friendship*, as an act of the will loving God as a *person*. It is an interpersonal union consisting of personal knowledge of God, which is primarily a social activity of the will in its capacity to love.[18]

---

[18] The best-known proponent of the intellectual model is Aquinas, and this way of understanding union with God is characteristic of the Dominican intellectual tradition. See especially Aquinas (1955:

It is important to point out that this question is not an either-or, because theists should agree that union with God involves both things. The debate is over which is *primary* in the sense of constituting the *essence* or *core* of union with God and being the *most valuable* activity that a human being can engage in. Is the fundamental act in which happiness consists better understood as the "vision of God" or the "love of God," contemplation or relationship? Is it more a union of knowledge or a union of love? Reflecting on the nature of union with God is important because, on the theistic perspective, it is the essence of true happiness and the best thing we can experience. But we do not have space to explore this issue in more depth. Having identified the dominant ways of understanding union with God, we will move on to the question of why it is considered the best thing for us.

3.4 Union with God as the Greatest Good

In this subsection, I will present an argument for the position that union with God is the supreme good. It is an argument from God's nature. Considerations of the divine nature are at the heart of most historically influential arguments for God as the *summum bonum* (see, for example, Calvin 1845; Augustine 1887a, 2012; Aquinas 1920, 1955; Anselm 2007a, 2007c). My argument can be seen as a "master argument" that contains elements of them and is based on the same central idea: the goodness of God. Here is the Master Argument:

1. The greatest good for human persons is to attain the highest degree of the fundamental intrinsic value(s) and the specific constituent(s) that contribute to happiness, whatever they are.
2. When human persons are united with God, they attain the goodness contained in the divine nature, to the extent that it is possible for them to do.
3. God's nature contains the highest degree of every kind of goodness, including the fundamental intrinsic value(s) and the specific constituent(s) that contribute to happiness, whatever they are.
4. So, when human persons are united with God, they attain the highest degree of the fundamental intrinsic value(s) and the specific constituent(s) that contribute to happiness, whatever they are.
C. Therefore, whatever happiness consists in, union with God is the greatest good for human persons.

Before examining this argument, we must make a clarification regarding its scope. Although theism says that union with God is the greatest good both in

---

Ch. 25, 26, 37); (1920: I, q. 26, a. 2, I-II, q. 3, a. 5, 8). The best-known proponent of the social model is Augustine, and this way of understanding union with God is characteristic of the Franciscan intellectual tradition. See especially Augustine (2006); (1887b: Ch. 11); (2012: Bk. X, Ch. 3). These interpretations are not accepted by all scholars, but I will not enter into this debate.

earthly life and in the afterlife (assuming there is one), the argument is referring to the *final* and *best* state of union with God, which according to most theistic traditions occurs only in the afterlife, that is, in the postmortem state known as heaven. We will return to this point in Section 4.

Premise 1 is a conceptual truth that is true by definition. Whatever it is that makes us happy and constitutes the happy life, realizing that good (or goods) to the highest level or largest amount will make us as happy as possible. To fill in this premise with more determinate content, we can take the leading theories of happiness from Section 2 as the main options for the *fundamental intrinsic value(s)* that are the nature of happiness, and the list of popular candidates for the *specific constituents* of happiness from Subsection 3.1 as the main options for the goods that make up the content of happiness. Spelled out in this way, premise 1 reads: The greatest good for human persons is to attain the highest degree of the fundamental intrinsic value(s) of pleasure, desire satisfaction, objective goods, nature fulfillment, or virtue (or some combination of them); and the highest degree of the specific constituents of pleasure, honor, life, health, beauty, knowledge, autonomy, achievement, virtue, relationships, etc. (or some combination of them).

One potential objection to the argument is that happiness is subjective in the metaethical sense and happiness claims are wholly a matter of personal opinion. If someone does not believe that union with God is the greatest good, then it is not the greatest good for that person. This objection, if correct, would undermine the assumption behind premise 1 and the rest of the argument that there are objective and universal truths about human happiness. But this objection fails because, as I argued in Section 2, if theism is true then metaethical subjectivism is false. Because this argument, like the rest of the Element, is presupposing the conditional truth of theism, premise 1 should be interpreted as stating an objective and universal truth about happiness.

It might be objected that premises 2 and 3 are false because God does not exist, or they are rationally unjustified because there is not sufficient reason to believe in God. On this way of reading the argument, these premises assert the proposition that God exists. Of course, if they are meant to be interpreted this way and God does not in fact exist, then they are false. But this would be a misunderstanding of the argument. As I explained in Section 1, the goal of this Element is not to prove God's existence or the rationality of theistic belief, but to assume theism for the purpose of exploring its implications for happiness. This argument is conditional on the truth of theism and takes God's existence as a background assumption. So the conclusion should be interpreted this way: If God exists, then God is the greatest good for human persons. An atheist can still believe the argument is sound. He or she would then hold the following view: If

God existed, then union with God would be the greatest good for us; but it is not possible to achieve our greatest good because God does not exist.

Premise 2 says that union with God enables human persons to participate in the goodness contained in the divine nature to the extent that it is possible for them to do, in a way that is consistent with their metaphysical nature as finite human beings and their individual measure of knowledge and love of God. God, being all loving and wanting all human persons to be happy, is willing to give them as much goodness as they are able and willing to receive. When people come to know and love God and share a relationship of interpersonal union with God, they have access to God's goodness and can experience it in every aspect of their being: intellectually, volitionally, socially, emotionally, and so on. This premise is neutral among the more specific ways of understanding the nature of union with God that were catalogued in Subsection 3.3.

For the remainder of this section, I will explain and defend the key premise 3 in depth. This premise assumes the traditional concept of God that was defined in Section 1. According to classical theism, one of God's essential attributes is perfect goodness, which includes the doctrine that God's nature is *goodness itself* – infinite and perfect goodness. God's status as the metaphysically ultimate and greatest conceivable being entails that he is the ultimate cause and source of all goodness, as well as the locus and standard of all goodness. All goodness has its origin and its destination in God: he is the fount and the final end, the source and the summit, of all value. Everything that is good comes from and is somehow found in God. As Augustine puts it, "The perfection of all our good things and our perfect good is God" (1887b: Ch. 8).

Augustine explains this idea philosophically by identifying what Plato calls the "Form of the Good" with God himself. The Platonic understanding of God's goodness is a popular one in the theistic tradition. Its most prominent contemporary defender is Robert Adams, who says that the proposition that "God is the supreme Good, and excellent without qualification, is a view I am confident that theists, at any rate, should hold. Indeed, it seems to be part of the package of views that define theism, if there is such a package" (1999: 28). According to Theistic Platonism, God is *The Good*: a transcendent good that is the paradigm of goodness. As Adams explains it, "The role that belongs to the Form of the Good in Plato's thought is assigned to God, and the goodness of other things is understood in terms of their standing in some relation, usually conceived as a sort of resemblance, to God" (1999: 14). On Adams's theory, goodness is understood as "excellence" or intrinsic value simpliciter. Creaturely excellence is analyzed as "resemblance" to the Good and thus resemblance to God: "other things are excellent insofar as they resemble or imitate God" (1999: 28–29).

There are other ways besides Theistic Platonism to analyze God's goodness, but we will not explore them here.[19] The leading approaches all maintain that God represents the *ideal* and *maximum* of goodness for *all* types of goodness, and that all real goods somehow *resemble* or *participate in* the goodness of God. This includes prudential goodness or happiness. God's nature represents the paradigm of happiness, and creaturely happiness is a participation in God's happiness. Union with God is the best state possible for a human being, whether happiness is considered as the fundamental good-makers that define its nature or the specific goods that make up its content. This is the justification for premise 3 in the argument.

We can go beyond this general answer and explain how God's nature represents the highest possible degree of the relevant intrinsic values and constituents, adding further support to premise 3. In Section 2 we briefly saw how God's goodness contains all the types of intrinsic goodness that define the five leading theories of happiness: pleasure, desire satisfaction, objective goods, nature fulfillment, and virtue. Can this be spelled out in more detail? Yes, with one caveat. Since the Master Argument is meant to cover *whatever it is* that makes up the true nature and content of happiness, a comprehensive and exhaustive defense of the argument would require an examination of every potential candidate for a fundamental intrinsic value and specific constituent. That would require much more space than I have here. Instead, I will use a set of goods that are widely considered to be major contributors to happiness. These goods frequently appear on lists of the content of happiness, and they have a place in many of the leading theories of the nature of happiness. For this reason, they are especially fitting to use for the purpose of illustration. My discussion will cover the goods of pleasure, virtue, desire satisfaction, nature fulfillment, friendship, knowledge, and beauty.

Before examining these goods, we must reintroduce an important conclusion from Section 2. There I argued that for theists the most plausible view of the nature of happiness will have an objective component and will not be purely subjective. Happiness does not come solely from a subjective mental state like pleasure or desire; instead, it is partly or wholly a matter of attaining objective goods, however they are understood (e.g., in an objective list, perfectionist, or eudaimonist way). On the theistic perspective, the most valuable sort of pleasure cannot be pleasure in just *any experience* a person might happen to enjoy

---

[19] For example, the Thomistic account understands God's goodness as metaphysical goodness or fullness of being and analyzes all other types of goodness as being grounded in metaphysical goodness and hence in God's being. See, for example, Aquinas (1920: I, q. 5); Stump and Kretzmann (1988).

(for example, morally depraved pleasures such as the delight in inflicting pain on others); instead, it must be pleasure *in what is objectively good*. Likewise, the most valuable sort of desire satisfaction cannot be the satisfaction of just *any desire* a person might happen to have (for example, self-destructive desires like the wish to abuse hard drugs); instead, it must be the satisfaction of desires *for what is objectively good*. As Augustine puts it, happy is the person who "both has whatsoever good things he wills and wills no evil ones" (1887a: Bk. XIII, Ch. 6). Happiness involves not simply getting whatever we want, but having what we want and wanting only things that are truly good (for further study, see Aquinas 1920: I-II, q. 1, a. 5; Budziszewski 2020: 642–644).

One reason theists should recognize an objective condition on happiness is that the essence of happiness is union with God, and God is objective goodness itself. Whatever is included in the state of union with God therefore must be compatible with God's essential goodness. Union with God is thus incompatible with pleasant experiences and satisfactions whose objects are not good. Enjoying or wanting something that is not good will prevent a person from being in union with God who is The Good. This conclusion has important implications for the theistic analysis of the subjective goods of pleasure and desire, as well as for other items on our list. Let us now examine each of these goods.

First, pleasure is an inevitable effect of union with God. When one is united to the source of all being and value – infinite and perfect goodness, truth, and beauty itself – the natural response will be enjoyment and delight. Union with God is the most pleasant experience possible. Calvin writes that in heaven "there will be so much pleasantness in the very sight [of God], so much delight in the very knowledge [of God], that this happiness will far surpass all the means of enjoyment which are now afforded" (1845: Bk. III, Ch. 25). Anselm argues that union with God brings maximal pleasure because God is the cause and exemplar of all goodness:

> For if particular goods are delightful, consider intently how delightful is that good which contains the joyfulness of all goods – and not such joyfulness as we have experienced in created things, but as different from that as the Creator differs from the creature. If created life is good, how good is the life that creates? If the salvation that has been brought about is joyful, how joyful is the salvation that brings about all salvation? If wisdom in the knowledge of created things is desirable, how desirable is the wisdom that created all things from nothing? In short, if there are many and great delights in delightful things, what kind and how great a delight is there in him who made those delightful things?" (2007c: Ch. 24)

Union with God is also the source and organizing principle of other pleasures. According to Jonathan Edwards,

[A]s it is with the love of the saints, so it is with their joy, and spiritual delight and pleasure: the first foundation of it is not any consideration or conception of their interest in divine things; but it primarily consists in the sweet entertainment their minds have in the view of contemplation of the divine and holy beauty of these things, as they are in themselves . . . . True saints have their minds, in the first place, inexpressibly pleased and delighted with the sweet ideas of the glorious and amiable nature of the things of God. And this is the spring of all their delights, and the cream of all their pleasures: it is the joy of their joy. (1746: Part III, Ch. 2)

Echoing Edwards, Jerry Walls says that "union with God is the central integrating pleasure of heaven and . . . all other things are enjoyed in such a way that God is recognized as their source and glorified thereby" (2002: 195).

Stuart Goetz, a theistic hedonist, describes perfect heavenly happiness as "the idea of an unending life (existence) that is filled with the best possible or optimal experiences of pleasure (assuming that there are such optimal experiences) and without any experiences of pain. Such a life is the happiest life possible . . . . this happiness extends indefinitely into the future and consists of nothing but experiences of pleasure" (2012: 10). This state of maximal pleasure with no pain is possible because God, who is omnipotent and omnibenevolent, has the power and the desire to actualize it for those who are in the immortal state of heavenly union with God. In that state, we will be immune from the obstacles to enjoyment and the sources of suffering that detract from our pleasure in this life, and our experience of heavenly pleasure will be continuous and everlasting.

Second, union with God involves the highest degree of virtue. Being virtuous involves having a *good will*: a will that wills, desires, chooses, and acts in accordance with what is truly good. Willing the good, having the other aspects of one's character integrated around a good will, and acting in accordance with it, are necessary conditions of virtue. Now, union among two persons involves a union of wills. To be united to God, a human person must will what God wills. God is essentially perfectly good and goodness itself, and God cannot contradict his own nature, so God always wills the good. Therefore, a human person in union with God also must will the good. Without a virtuous character a person cannot will what God wills and thus cannot be in a state of right relationship with God. Just as moral wrongdoing against a friend damages or destroys a human friendship, moral wrongdoing strains or ruptures one's relationship with God, causing one to be alienated from God and thus in a state of unhappiness.

In fact, *perfect* union with God – the highest possible degree of happiness – requires *perfect* virtue – perfectly willing what God wills. Since God wills only the good, to be fully united to God a human person must will the good whole-heartedly and impeccably, which means that she must be fully virtuous because the essence of virtue is having a good will that is rightly ordered and wills the good. It is impossible for such a person to will, enjoy, or desire evil, or to be vicious or commit morally bad actions, because doing so is incompatible with being in perfect union with God. Hence, union with God involves the highest degree of virtue (for further study, see Aquinas 1920: I-II, q. 4, a. 4; Stump 2010: Ch. 5–8).[20]

The third item on our list is desire satisfaction. As I have argued, theism implies that happiness is not totally subjective in nature, and some things – most importantly union with God – are objectively good for us independently of our desires. God created us for the purpose of being happy by attaining the objective good of a loving relationship with him. In light of this, it is plausible to think that God designed human nature in such a way that our desires naturally (but not infallibly) direct us toward what is good, which is ultimately the same thing as saying that they direct us toward God who is The Good. For example, the human mind is naturally structured so that belief aims at truth, and the human will is naturally structured so that (rational) desire aims at goodness.[21] It is extremely implausible to suppose that God designed us so that our natural desires are aimed at things that are objectively bad. Hence, theism supports the idea that there are natural and universal human desires for things that are objectively good, such as friendship, knowledge, and beauty. These can be understood as either actual desires that people do have, or idealized desires that people would have if they were fully informed and rational.

This account of desire is relevant to the explanation of why union with God brings the fullest satisfaction of desire, which is itself connected to the explanation of why union with God brings maximal nature fulfillment and participation in objective goods like friendship, knowledge, and beauty. My way of spelling out these points will draw upon two influential historical arguments for the position that union with God is the greatest good, which come from Augustine and Aquinas.

Augustine's *Confessions* is a compelling narrative argument that union with God is the only thing that can completely satisfy our desires and fulfill our nature. The main theme of the book is stated in the famous line at the beginning, when Augustine says to God: "Thou hast made us for Thyself, and our hearts are restless till they rest in Thee" (2006: Bk. I, Ch. 1). On his philosophical

---

[20] Most theists have a conception of virtue that includes theological aspects, which affects how they understand the virtue-dimension of happiness. According to Christian theism, for example, knowing and loving God requires that one possess the "theological virtues" of faith, hope, and charity, which are the most important virtues. Because they essentially involve God in various ways, the highest form of virtue will be irreducibly theological in character. I do not have space to explore specific accounts of virtue in this Element, however.

[21] This is typically coupled with the "guise of the good" thesis that we always desire something under the aspect of goodness; everything we rationally desire is something we consider to be good in some way, whether its goodness is real or merely apparent. If this is a fact of human psychology, theism explains it.

anthropology, human beings have been created to know and love God. We cannot be fulfilled by anything else, no matter how good it is, and we will always be unsatisfied until we experience friendship with God, which is the best form of friendship. Augustine's life can be seen as a quest to find happiness in all the wrong places, pursuing false goods and putting lesser goods above greater goods, culminating in his realization that only a loving relationship with God will quiet his restless heart. The truth, goodness, and beauty that he seeks throughout his life ultimately lead him to God, who is truth, goodness, and beauty themselves. Augustine's life is a testament to Shakespeare's line that "Men's natures wrangle with inferior things, though great ones are their object" (2008a: 5.2.368–369). The *Confessions* is Augustine's spiritual autobiography and the story of a soul; but it is also meant to be the story of every human soul. Friendship with God is the purpose of human life and the thing that brings us true happiness, puts our heart's desires to rest, and fulfills our nature in the fullest way possible.

As Augustine sees it, our "restless heart" – the fact that we constantly desire and seek happiness and fulfillment but cannot achieve it apart from God – is a good thing that is part of God's design. This point is illustrated beautifully in George Herbert's poem "The Pulley":

> When God at first made man,
> Having a glasse of blessings standing by;
> Let us (said he) poure on him all we can:
> Let the worlds riches, which dispersed lie,
> Contract into a span.
>
> So strength first made a way;
> Then beautie flow'd, then wisdome, honour, pleasure:
> When almost all was out, God made a stay,
> Perceiving that alone of all his treasure
> Rest in the bottome lay.
>
> For if I should (said he)
> Bestow this jewell also on my creature,
> He would adore my gifts in stead of me,
> And rest in Nature, not the God of Nature:
> So both should losers be.
>
> Yet let him keep the rest,
> But keep them with repining restlesnesse:
> Let him be rich and wearie, that at least,
> If goodnesse leade him not, yet wearinesse
> May tosse him to my breast.
> (2016: 127)

On the theistic view articulated by Augustine and Herbert, it is natural for us to desire God and seek God because in so doing we are acting in accordance with our nature and pursuing that which will achieve our purpose of being happy. Our "repining restlessness" and our natural desires for things like friendship and knowledge will, if followed to completion, lead us to God. And union with God will perfect our nature and bring the total fulfillment and satisfaction we seek.

We can expand on the line of thought that the *Confessions* articulates narratively and philosophically. As I argued in Section 1, according to theism, God created human beings with a certain nature and for a certain purpose. God is also essentially perfectly good, which has two significant corollaries. One is that God wills the good of every creature he has made, and thus wills their happiness. The other is that God is the most valuable thing that human beings can unite with. If we follow Augustine in assuming that the highest degree of happiness consists in possessing and being united to the highest kind of goodness, it entails that God himself is the highest good for human beings. God therefore must will that every human person be united to him. God created humanity for the purpose of being maximally happy in eternal union with himself.

Aquinas's argument is in the same spirit as Augustine's, and it too focuses on human desire and human nature, but its style and emphasis are different. He presents a philosophical case that "man's last end is the uncreated good, namely, God, who alone by his infinite goodness can perfectly satisfy man's will" (1920: I-II, q. 3, a. 1). Here is Aquinas's central argument that true happiness is found in union with God:

> It is impossible for any created good to constitute man's happiness. For happiness is the perfect good, which lulls the appetite altogether; else it would not be the last end, if something yet remained to be desired. Now the object of the will, i.e., of man's appetite, is the universal good, just as the object of the intellect is the universal true. Hence it is evident that naught can lull man's will, save the universal good. This is to be found, not in any creature, but in God alone, because every creature has goodness by participation. Wherefore God alone can satisfy the will of man, according to the words of Psalm 102:5: "Who satisfieth thy desire with good things." Therefore, God alone constitutes man's happiness. (1920: I-II, q. 2, a. 8)

This passage focuses on the notion of goodness, but Aquinas's reasoning applies to truth as well. The Thomistic argument can be formulated as follows:

1. Happiness is the perfect good that fully satisfies our desires.
2. We have a desire for complete and perfect goodness because the object of the human will is the "universal good."

3. We have a desire for complete and perfect truth because the object of the human intellect is the "universal true."
4. So, only complete and perfect goodness and truth can bring us happiness.
5. God alone is complete and perfect goodness and truth.
C. Therefore, God alone can bring us happiness.

Premise 1 assumes that the satisfaction of all (natural) desires is a necessary condition for happiness. If we are left wanting more, we will not be happy. The argument is framed in terms of desire, but it also involves objective goods (goodness and truth) and human perfection: union with God is what objectively fulfills human nature to the fullest extent possible. Premises 2 and 3 are based on Aquinas's philosophical anthropology, which affirms the account of desire I laid out earlier. On his understanding of human nature, the essential human capacities are the rational capacities of intellect and will, whose objects are, respectively, truth and goodness. Every human being has a natural desire for truth and goodness because they are the natural ends that fulfill our intellectual and volitional powers. Furthermore, these desires will not be satisfied by any finite and limited amount of truth and goodness. No matter how much we attain, we will still be left wanting more, and these desires can be quenched only if we reach a kind of truth and goodness that is infinite and unlimited – *truth and goodness themselves as such*. The nature of the human mind and will are such that we do not just want to know some truths and love some goods, but *all* truth and *all* goodness.

Premise 5 says that these things are found in God alone. According to classical theism, God's nature is truth itself and goodness itself. Thus, it is only through union with God that we can fully satisfy our desires for objective truth and goodness and fulfill our nature. When we experience union with God, we are guaranteed to be happy because every sort of truth and goodness that we can desire will be found in the divine nature. As Dante expresses it: "He who beholds that Light is so enthralled that he would never willingly consent to turn away from it for any other sight, because the good that is the object of the will is held and gathered in perfection there, that elsewhere would imperfect show" (2008: XXXIII, 100–105).

These Augustinian and Thomistic arguments, if successful, show that union with God is the pinnacle of human happiness because it involves the highest degree of desire satisfaction, human fulfillment, objective goodness, friendship, and knowledge.

The last good we will explore is beauty. Along with truth and goodness, beauty is one of the three primary "transcendentals" – features or attributes that can be said of all existing things – recognized throughout the history of philosophy.[22] Just as our deepest desires for truth and goodness are fulfilled in God, whose nature is truth itself and goodness itself, the same can be said about our desire for beauty. Because God's goodness contains every kind of value, including aesthetic value, God is also beauty itself and the source and archetype of all beauty.

The most famous philosophical expression of the idea that beauty is divine is found in Plato's *Symposium*. The climax of the dialogue is the character Diotima's speech about love, in which she explains the "ladder of love" representing the stages of the knowledge and love of beauty. According to Plato (speaking through Diotima), one begins with a love of particular beautiful things, and from there one ascends up the ladder until one arrives at a love of beauty itself, "at the notion of absolute beauty, and at last knows what the essence of beauty is" (1956: 211c). In the final stage,

> drawing towards and contemplating the vast sea of beauty . . . at last the vision is revealed to him . . . [and] when he comes toward the end [he] will suddenly perceive a nature of wondrous beauty . . . a nature which in the first place is everlasting, not growing and decaying, or waxing and waning; secondly, not fair in one point of view and foul in another, or at one time or in one relation or at one place fair, at another time or in another relation or at another place foul, as if fair to some and foul to others, or in the likeness of a face or hands or any other part of the bodily frame, or in any form of speech or knowledge, or existing in any other being, as for example, in an animal, or in heaven, or in earth, or in any other place; but beauty absolute, separate, simple, and everlasting, which without diminution and without increase, or any change, is imparted to the ever-growing and perishing beauties of all other things. (1956: 210d–211b)

Diotima says that "if man had eyes to see the true beauty – the divine beauty, I mean, pure and clear and unalloyed, not clogged with the pollutions of mortality and all the colours and vanities of human life," it would be "that life above all others which man should live, in the contemplation of beauty absolute" (1956: 211d–211e). As Plato sees it, the ladder of love leads a person to happiness through contemplative union with the divine Platonic Form of The Beautiful.

Plato's view naturally lends itself to a theistic interpretation that locates the Form of Beauty in God and understands God's nature as beauty itself. This is why Augustine often addresses God by the name "Beauty," as in his poignant and memorable cry: "Late have I loved Thee, O Beauty so ancient and so new; late have I loved Thee!" (2006: Bk. X, Ch. 27). When we experience the beatific

---

[22] These are not the only transcendentals. The traditional list includes being, goodness, truth, unity, *res* (thing), and *aliquid* (something). Beauty was not a distinct item on the original list but was added later.

vision of God, our reaction will be like that of Augustine recognizing God as The Beautiful. Or, if one is fond of Shakespeare, it will be like that of Romeo after seeing Juliet for the first time: "Did my heart love till now? Forswear it, sight, For I ne'er saw true beauty till this night" (2008b: 1.5.49–50). Or, if one prefers Dante, our experience of God's beauty will be even more overwhelming and ineffable than Dante's reaction to seeing his beloved Beatrice in her radiant heavenly glory, which pushed him beyond his conceptual and linguistic limits: "The beauty that I saw transcends all thought of beauty, and I must believe that only its maker may savor it all. I declare myself defeated at this point more than any poet, whether comic or tragic, was ever thwarted by a topic in his theme, for, like sunlight striking on the weakest eyes, the memory of the sweetness of that smile deprives me of my mental powers" (2008: XXX, 19–27). No matter which poetic expression we prefer, the upshot is that union with God involves the fullest participation in the good of beauty, the last item on our list.

This ends our analysis of the specific ways in which union with God brings the highest realization of pleasure, virtue, desire satisfaction, nature fulfillment, friendship, knowledge, and beauty. Even after this lengthy examination of some leading candidates for the fundamental intrinsic values and specific constituents of happiness, a final objection might be raised. It could be alleged that the preceding discussion leaves out the correct theory of the nature of happiness, which is not one of the five leading theories covered in this Element, and/or it neglects some good that is a crucial ingredient of happiness. In reply, it is true that my argument is limited in the number of goods it covers, for the simple reason that it is not possible to cover them all in this short work. But in the end, the objection is doomed to fail no matter which good is put forward as the missing one. Any other candidate for a fundamental intrinsic value or a specific constituent can be plugged into the argument and it will still succeed because this other good – if it is a real good – will be included in premise 3 of the Master Argument. No matter how the details are spelled out, it will be one of the goods contained in the divine nature, which encompasses every real good there is.

In summary, the reasoning of the Master Argument is that because God is goodness itself, all goods are found in God in their fullest and most perfect form. All finite goodness resembles and participates in the infinite divine goodness. Whatever contributes to happiness as an intrinsic value or a specific constituent is fully realized in union with God. Pleasure, desire, objective goods, human fulfillment, and virtue, along with more specific goods that are parts of a happy life, have their ultimate end and highest perfection in God. Thus, no matter which theory of the nature and content of happiness is correct, union with God will be the best thing for us.

Before ending our discussion of the Master Argument, we should ask if there is any other supporting evidence for its premises aside from the conditional assumption of theism, conceptual truths about happiness and the divine attributes, the various propositions I have inferred from them, the arguments of Augustine and Aquinas, and the arguments from authority and arguments by example that I have given. The answer is yes. Roughly speaking, there are two main ways to evaluate philosophical claims and positions: theoretically using rational argument, and practically using personal experience. Evidence comes in the form of both arguments (a third-personal approach) and experiences (a first-personal approach).[23]

Both logical reasoning and phenomenological introspection are necessary when reflecting on the topic of human happiness. In addition to evaluating the arguments for and against the various theses and theories we have covered, we can also test them against the data of experience. This point applies in a special way to the topics discussed in this section, especially the proposition that union with God is the supreme good that brings maximal happiness, and the claims about human nature and desire contained in the Master Argument. It may be that these claims cannot be evaluated solely on the basis of theoretical arguments that appeal to abstract propositions and rational intuitions; instead, they must also be confirmed or disconfirmed by lived experience. For instance, regarding the claim that only union with God will fully satisfy our desires and bring our hearts to rest, the best way to test it could be honest introspection and self-examination, which has been central to the practice of philosophy since the ancient thinkers adopted as their motto the famous decree of the Oracle at Delphi: "Know thyself." It is supposed to be a claim about human nature, and we can evaluate it both by rational reflection and argument, and by critical reflection on our human experience, looking into our own hearts the way Augustine does in the *Confessions*.

3.5 Conclusion

This section has explored the content and structure of happiness, focusing on the specific good of religion and the central theistic claim that union with God is the *summum bonum* and the pinnacle of happiness. We have surveyed different ways of understanding the nature of union with God, and we have examined an argument for the position that it is the greatest good for human beings. But there is an important question remaining. *Can* we achieve union with God? Is the theistic ideal of happiness even *possible*? This question will be taken up in the next section.

---

[23] The way I am framing it is meant to be generic and nonpartisan in its epistemological commitments, not dependent on any specific theory of epistemic rationality, justification, or evidence.

4 The Possibility of Happiness

The previous sections investigated the concept of happiness, the nature of happiness, and the constituents of a happy life. Even if all these questions have been answered, there is another crucial one remaining: *Can we be happy? Is happiness possible* for human beings? The sort of possibility I have in mind is realizability in the actual world (not some possible world different from the one we inhabit), where the actual world includes both earthly life and the afterlife (if one exists).[24] Is happiness something we can experience, given the facts about human nature and the world as we find them? Can you and I – the real individuals who exist in this world – be happy? In tackling this question, first we will examine a key distinction between perfect and imperfect happiness. Then we will compare theism and atheism regarding the possibility of happiness.

4.1 Perfect and Imperfect Happiness

In the history of philosophy, there is an important distinction between two sorts of happiness: *perfect happiness* and *imperfect happiness*. One of its first clear and explicit statements is found in Aquinas, who takes himself to be synthesizing and developing the ideas of earlier thinkers, especially Aristotle, Augustine, and Boethius. Drawing upon this historical stream, I will lay out my own version of the distinction, which will be used throughout this section.

First, perfect happiness is happiness in an *unqualified* sense, whereas imperfect happiness is happiness in a *qualified* sense. As Aquinas puts it, "man's happiness is twofold, one perfect, the other imperfect. And by perfect happiness we are to understand that which attains to the true notion of happiness; and by imperfect happiness that which does not attain thereto but partakes of some particular likeness of happiness" (1920: I-II, q. 3, a. 6).

Next, perfect happiness is *complete* and *permanent*, whereas imperfect happiness is *incomplete* and *impermanent*. This includes both fullness and fixedness: perfect happiness has everything and is everlasting, it is all-inclusive and abiding.

---

[24] There are different ways to spell out the modality I am referring to in this section, which will determine the technical and precise meaning of "possible" and "impossible." In general, the sort of modality I have in mind includes the alethic (logical, conceptual, metaphysical, and nomic/physical/natural) and the epistemic. But I am leaving it imprecise because there is dispute about which kinds of modality are real and fundamental. Likewise, there are competing theories of modal metaphysics and semantics, and different ways to analyze and formulate modal claims such as "My happiness is possible." In terms of possible worlds, it might be: "There is a possible world in which I am happy, and this possible world could be the actual world." In terms of states of affairs, it might be: "The state of affairs of my being happy is actualizable in the actual world." I will use both kinds of language without committing to any theory of modality. My concern is realizability in our world, however this sense of possibility is spelled out.

To say that happiness is complete is to say that it is comprehensive and includes all prudential goods. In order to be perfectly happy, one must possess all basic intrinsic goods and lack no basic intrinsic goods. This condition is emphasized by Boethius, who writes that perfect happiness,

> is in fact the highest of all good things and it contains all good things within itself; if anything could be added to it, it could not be the highest good, since there would remain something external to it that could still be hoped for. It is therefore clear that happiness is a state brought about by the convergence of all good things. (2001: Bk. III, Prose 2)

To say that happiness is permanent is to say that it is stable, secure, unending, and unable to be lost. Aquinas maintains that,

> man naturally desires to hold to the good that he has, and to have the surety of his holding, or else he must of necessity be troubled with the fear of losing it, or with the sorrow of knowing that he will lose it. Therefore, it is necessary for true happiness that man have the assured opinion of never losing the good that he possesses. (1920: I-II, q. 5, a. 4)

Another condition for perfect happiness is *purity*, meaning happiness that is uncorrupted and untainted by moral or natural evils. Aquinas writes that "a perfect good is one which lacks any admixture of evil, just as a perfectly white thing is completely unmixed with black" (1955: Bk. III, Ch. 48). Imperfect happiness, by contrast, is impure and mixed with bad things.

A final feature of perfect happiness is *self-sufficiency*: it satisfies all of our desires, or, as many thinkers qualify it, all of our natural and properly ordered desires for things that are objectively good (or at least not bad).[25] "It is therefore necessary," says Aquinas, "for the last end so to fill man's appetite that nothing is left besides it for man to desire" (1920: I-II, q. 1, a. 5). Imperfect happiness is marked by the frustration of some (properly ordered) desires.

In summary, we can distinguish between happiness that is perfect, unqualified, complete, permanent, pure, and self-sufficient, and happiness that is imperfect, qualified, incomplete, impermanent, impure, and insufficient. With this distinction in hand, we can identify three main positions on the possibility of human happiness:[26]

---

[25] We encountered this view in previous sections, where it was argued that theists should affirm an objective condition on the value of desire satisfaction.

[26] These are not all the logically possible options, but they are the most significant ones. I follow Austin Fagothey (1959: Ch. 3) in naming the two general views "optimism" and "pessimism," but I define them differently and add the third mixed position. Fagothey says that the position one endorses will "depend chiefly on one's convictions about the existence of God and the immortality of the human soul" (1959: 48). I agree, and this will be illustrated in what follows.

(1) *Optimism*: perfect happiness and imperfect happiness are both possible.

(2) *Mixed pessimism and optimism*: perfect happiness is impossible but imperfect happiness is possible.

(3) *Pessimism*: perfect happiness and imperfect happiness are both impossible.

In what follows, we will explore the difference God makes to the possibility of happiness by comparing atheism and theism.

4.2 Atheism and the Possibility of Happiness

Two influential atheistic thinkers – Arthur Schopenhauer and Bertrand Russell – are representative of atheistic perspectives on the possibility of happiness. Schopenhauer, the quintessential philosopher of pessimism, unsurprisingly defends the pessimistic position that no real happiness is possible for human beings. He describes the human condition this way:

> [The human will's] desires are limitless, its claims inexhaustible, and every satisfied desire gives rise to a new one. No possible satisfaction in the world could suffice to still its longings, set a goal to its infinite cravings, and fill the bottomless abyss of its heart. Then let one consider what as a rule are the satisfactions of any kind that a man obtains. For the most part, nothing more than the bare maintenance of this existence itself, extorted day by day with unceasing trouble and constant care in the conflict with want, and with death in prospect. Everything in life shows that earthly happiness is destined to be frustrated or recognized as an illusion ... [T]hat continual illusion and disillusion, and also the nature of life throughout, presents itself to us as intended and calculated to awaken the conviction that nothing at all is worth our striving, our efforts and struggles, that all good things are vanity, the world and all its ends bankrupt, and life a business which does not cover its expenses. (2008: 114–115)

Schopenhauer continues:

> The way in which this vanity of all objects of the will makes itself known ... is primarily time. It is the form by means of which the vanity of things appears as their perishableness; for on account of this all our pleasures and joys disappear in our hands .... Thus old age and death, to which every life necessarily hurries on, are the sentence of condemnation on the will to live, coming from the hands of nature itself, and which declares that this will is an effort which frustrates itself. "What thou hast wished," it says, "ends thus: desire something better." Hence the instruction which his life affords to every one consists, as a whole, in this, that the objects of his desires continually delude, waver, and fall, and accordingly bring more misery than joy, till at last the whole foundation upon which they all stand gives way, in that his life itself is destroyed and so he receives the last proof that all his striving and wishing was a perversity, a false path. (2008: 115)

In depressing detail, Schopenhauer catalogs the various evils, miseries, and sufferings that permeate human life, along with the vanity, taintedness, and emptiness of human desires and goods. He also identifies time and mortality as the great enemies of happiness, because death brings a permanent and inescapable end to everything.

Russell has a less negative outlook than Schopenhauer and endorses the mixed position that is partly pessimistic and partly optimistic. On the one hand, he believes that a genuine form of happiness is attainable. For him, a happy life is one that includes enjoyment, knowledge, health, successful work, love and affection, serving noble causes, a sense of purpose, self-integration, and moral goodness (Russell 1930). According to Russell, "Fundamental happiness depends more than anything else upon what may be called a friendly interest in persons and things," which he calls "zest for life" (1930: 155, Ch. 11). The key to happiness is to direct one's affections and interests outward rather than inward in a self-centered and self-absorbed way. In short, "The happy man is the man who lives objectively, who has free affections and wide interests, who secures his happiness through these interests and affections and through the fact that they, in turn, make him an object of interest and affection to many others" (1930: 244). Dissenting from Schopenhauer's view that death precludes happiness, Russell claims that "Happiness is none the less true happiness because it must come to an end, nor do thought and love lose their value because they are not everlasting" (2004: 7). He is under no illusion that happiness is guaranteed, because it is partly beyond human control and there are plenty of unhappy lives. But he believes it is possible because many people have achieved it (including him).

On the other hand, Russell recognizes that such happiness is imperfect, and that perfect happiness is impossible. He writes: "The life of Man is a long march through the night, surrounded by invisible foes, tortured by weariness and pain, towards a goal that few can hope to reach, and where none may tarry long. One by one, as they march, our comrades vanish from our sight, seized by the silent orders of omnipotent Death" (1999: 38). As an atheist, Russell believes that we live in an impersonal and inhospitable cosmos; the universe is not a friendly home that is designed with human happiness in mind:

> Brief and powerless is Man's life; on him and all his race the slow, sure doom falls pitiless and dark. Blind to good and evil, reckless of destruction, omnipotent matter rolls on its relentless way; for Man, condemned today to lose his dearest, tomorrow himself to pass through the gate of darkness, it remains only to cherish, ere yet the blow falls, the lofty thoughts that ennoble his little day. (1999: 38)

Russell draws the following moral:

> To every man comes, sooner or later, the great renunciation. For the young, there is nothing unattainable; a good thing desired with the whole force of a passionate will, and yet impossible, is to them not credible. Yet, by death, by illness, by poverty, or by the voice of duty, we must learn, each one of us, that the world was not made for us, and that, however beautiful may be the things we crave, Fate may nevertheless forbid them. (1999: 35)

The solution Russell recommends is resignation and acceptance that the perfect happiness we seek is impossible. He says, "Let us preserve our respect for truth, for beauty, for the ideal of perfection which life does not permit us to attain, though none of these things meet with the approval of the unconscious universe" (1999: 34). Russell poetically concludes: "To abandon the struggle for private happiness, to expel all eagerness of temporary desire, to burn with passion for eternal things – this is emancipation, and this is the free man's worship" (1999: 37).

Most contemporary atheistic philosophers probably agree with Russell's view that imperfect happiness is possible but precarious, and perfect happiness is unattainable. In a Godless world, some kind of happiness is available to us, but it is flawed, fragile, fleeting, and far from guaranteed. The best we can hope for in this life (which is the only life there is) is imperfect happiness, if we are fortunate and if the world and other people cooperate.

Following these thinkers, let us summarize the main reasons why perfect happiness is impossible during earthly life.

(1) Pleasure: the large amount of time when we are unable to enjoy ourselves, the fact that pleasing things become boring and unenjoyable after they have lost their luster, and frequent painful experiences.
(2) Desire: the frustration of many of our desires, and the unending and unquenchable desire for something more and something better.
(3) Objective goods: the fragility, instability, contingency, and finiteness of all earthly goods.
(4) Human fulfillment: the flaws of nature, the limitations and malfunctions of our natural powers, and the phenomena of vulnerability, dependence, disease, and impairment.
(5) Virtue: human fallibility, bad natural dispositions of intellect and will, moral imperfection and proneness to moral wrongdoing, the never-ending battle against vice, and the moral horrors that human beings inflict on one another.
(6) Death: the fact that all happiness is transient, and the long, dark shadow of impermanence that mortality casts across earthly life, along with its ensuing fear, despair, and existential angst.

(7) Suffering: the inescapability, amount, duration, variety, and intensity of human suffering, which is connected to all of the previous items.

These obstacles to happiness can be boiled down to two things: the absence of good and the presence of evil. In the next subsection, we will see how they can be overcome on a theistic worldview.

4.3 Theism and the Possibility of Happiness

Theism takes the optimistic position that perfect happiness and imperfect happiness are both possible (but not necessary or guaranteed). In contrast to the atheistic perspective, where the best we can hope for is imperfect happiness, theism allows for the possibility of perfect happiness. Here we must make another important distinction between happiness in earthly life and happiness in the afterlife, which are two different segments of a person's whole life. On the theistic view, it is possible to be happy in this life, but it will be imperfect. Perfect happiness is attainable only in the life to come. As Aquinas puts it, "A certain participation of happiness can be had in this life, but perfect and true happiness cannot be had in this life" (1920: I-II, q. 5, a. 3).[27]

To be more specific, perfect happiness is found only in the good postmortem state known as heaven. There is much that can be said about heaven and the afterlife, but I will limit my discussion to the points that are necessary for the purposes of this section. The essence of heaven is union with God, which is why it is necessarily a happy state.[28] As we saw in Section 3, on the theistic perspective the essence of happiness and the greatest good for human persons is knowing and loving God. Imperfect happiness is primarily a matter of knowing and loving God in this life, which is imperfect because our knowledge, love, and intellectual and personal union with God is suboptimal. Perfect happiness is primarily a matter of knowing and loving God in the next life, which is perfect because our knowledge, love, and intellectual and personal union with God is optimal. The perfect happiness of heaven is both *quantitatively* and *qualitatively* superior to the imperfect happiness of earth. As Jerry Walls explains, "Such happiness is not merely a quantitative thing. It is not merely a matter of having the opportunity to enjoy more finite goods for a longer time.

---

[27] Recall the distinction between momentary happiness and lifetime happiness from Section 1. The claims made here concern the momentary happiness of earthly life and the afterlife. We can add a claim about lifetime happiness that is widely accepted by theists: someone who experiences perfect happiness in the afterlife will for that reason have an overall happy life, because the value of perfect happiness is so great that it outweighs any earthly unhappiness and makes one's life good on the whole.

[28] See Walls (2002: 3–13) for a helpful overview of the major conceptions of heaven found in the Christian tradition. As Walls notes, the dominant one is the "theocentric" model on which the essence of heaven is the beatific vision or union with God.

Rather, it is a matter of knowing complete satisfaction by achieving union with the boundless source of happiness who lies behind all finite goods" (2002: 195). The reason is that God is both an *infinite* good that is quantitatively greater than any finite created good, and a *perfect* good that is qualitatively better than any imperfect created good. As Anselm poignantly expresses it, "if particular goods are delightful, consider intently how delightful is that good which contains the joyfulness of all goods – and not such joyfulness as we have experienced in created things, but as different from that as the Creator differs from the creature" (2007c: Ch. 24).

Theism can overcome all the obstacles to perfect happiness that were identified in the previous subsection. One major problem is the absence of goodness, which pertains to all the fundamental intrinsic values. In the conditions of earthly life, our experience of pleasure, satisfaction of desire, participation in objective goods, fulfillment of human nature, and cultivation of virtue are limited, unstable, and defective in myriad ways. At best, we can attain a less-than-perfect form and a less-than-maximal degree of happiness. To see how theism solves this problem, recall from Section 3 that union with God, whose nature is goodness itself, represents the pinnacle of goodness according to every theory of value. The five potential paths to perfect happiness all end in God. Whether we understand perfect happiness in terms of maximal pleasure, complete satisfaction of desire, utmost participation in objective goods, full human flourishing, or perfect virtue, heavenly union with God will provide it. For a person united to God in the heavenly state, no real good can be lacking because God is The Good who contains all goodness whatsoever. This is one way in which heavenly union with God brings perfect happiness.

Theism also overcomes the second major obstacle to perfect happiness: the presence of evil. After stating that perfect happiness cannot be had in this life, Aquinas gives one reason why: "For since happiness is a 'perfect and sufficient good,' it excludes every evil, and fulfils every desire. But in this life every evil cannot be excluded. For this present life is subject to many unavoidable evils" (1920: I-II, q. 5, a. 3). The three greatest impediments to earthly happiness are vice, suffering, and death. None will exist in heaven, which by definition is a state of perfect and everlasting happiness containing no moral or natural evil, no vice or immorality, no pain or suffering, and no decay or death. God is able to solve the problem of evil and defeat the sufferings of this life, which undermine human happiness in so many ways, by redeeming them and ultimately bringing good out of evil. Without positing God and an afterlife, it is unlikely that some instances of human suffering can be defeated (see Walls 2002: Ch. 5; Stump 2010).

Aquinas gives another reason why perfect happiness is impossible in this life: "neither can the desire for good be satiated in this life. For man naturally desires the good, which he has, to be abiding. Now the goods of the present life pass away, since life itself passes away" (1920: I-II, q. 5, a. 3). In asserting the requirement of immortality for perfect happiness, Aquinas is drawing on a long thread in the Western philosophical tradition. Many thinkers have held that permanence and stability are necessary conditions for true happiness, and they require immortality. Plato, for example, argues that human beings naturally desire to possess the good forever, and therefore to be immortal. In the *Symposium*, he suggests that the object of love is the good, and that we want the things we love to be ours eternally: "In a word, then, love is wanting to possess the good forever" (1997: 206a). From this, Plato concludes that "A lover must desire immortality along with the good" (1997: 207a).

Augustine gives several arguments for the position that happiness requires immortality. In the *City of God*, he writes:

> [E]ven the righteous man will not live as he wishes unless he reaches a state where he cannot possibly die, be deceived, or suffer harm, and where he is completely certain that this will always be so. For this is our nature's aim, and it will not be fully and perfectly happy unless it attains its aim. But who is now able to live as he wishes to live when life itself is not in his power? He wants to live, but he is compelled to die. How can he live as he wishes when he cannot even live as long as he wishes? . . . . If a person does not love his happy life, he obviously does not have the happy life . . . if it is loved as fully as it deserves to be loved (for no one is happy who does not love the happy life itself as fully as it deserves to be loved), the person who loves it so much cannot help but want it to be eternal. Thus the happy life will only be truly happy when it is eternal. (2012: Bk. XIV, Ch. 25)

Later theistic philosophers endorse this position, too. As we have seen, Aquinas maintains that "perfect and true happiness requires that one should be certain of being happy for ever, else the will would not rest" (1920: II-II, q. 18, a. 3). And Calvin says that "everything longs for permanent existence. I admit this, and therefore contend that we ought to look to future immortality, where we may obtain that fixed condition which nowhere appears on the earth" (1845: Bk. III, Ch. 9).

At this point, we need to clarify the logical connection between God's existence and the afterlife. Strictly speaking, theism does not logically entail immortality, nor does atheism entail the lack of immortality. But these positions usually go hand in hand, and it is a fairly short logical path from theism to immortality. Here is one line of reasoning to get there. Given God's nature as the omnipotent creator of all things, God would be *able* to secure human immortality. Given God's nature as all good and all loving, God would *want* to do so, because death is an evil and an afterlife in which human beings are eternally perfectly happy is a good, and perfect happiness in heaven is better than imperfect happiness or no happiness on earth. Hence, God would actualize the better state of affairs that includes a heavenly afterlife.

This leads us to a final point about theism and the possibility of happiness. If God exists, then perfect happiness is not just a *mere* possibility but also a *reality*. It is something that not only can exist in some possible world but does (or will) exist in our actual world. I will offer a brief defense of this claim.

In Section 1, I argued that all human beings want to be happy and that God wants us to be happy. Now I will go a step further and say that God wants us to be *perfectly* happy. This conclusion can be derived from the divine attributes, especially God's status as creator and his perfect goodness. If God is all good and all loving, then he wills the highest good for every person he has made. The highest good for a person is perfect happiness. So, God must will the perfect happiness of every created person. On a theistic perspective, one of God's purposes in creating human beings is for us to be perfectly happy in heavenly union with him.

It is important to clarify that God's primary purpose is for us to be happy *in the life to come*. God does want us to be imperfectly happy in this life, but this is secondary and subordinate to his chief purpose of perfect happiness in the next life. God's overriding and strongest desire for us is perfect heavenly happiness, not imperfect earthly happiness. Because he wills our good, God also wills for us to be happy on earth, provided it is compatible with and conducive toward the union with God that will bring perfect happiness in heaven. But the two do not always go together, and sometimes God allows human beings to experience earthly unhappiness because it is the best or only way to secure their perfect happiness.[29]

We can use these assumptions about God's nature and will, along with the assumption of God's existence (which is being assumed throughout this Element), to construct an argument for the conclusion that perfect happiness is a reality rather than a mere unactualized possibility. From the fact that our all-good and all-powerful creator desires our perfect happiness, it can be inferred that perfect human happiness is a *"real* possibility," that is, a state of affairs that *can and will* be actualized in our world. Put differently, on a theistic perspective, the actual world is one where at least some human beings will experience perfect happiness.[30] If we denied that perfect happiness is a reality, we would have to say

---

[29] For a magisterial theodicy along these lines, which holds that suffering is the best or only means available to bring (at least many) free human persons into loving union with God, see Stump (2010).

[30] I am *not* claiming that all human persons *actually will* be perfectly happy (or imperfectly happy). There is a debate among theists, especially adherents of Christian, Jewish, and Islamic theism, over how many human persons will experience perfect happiness in heaven. As far as I am aware, no theistic tradition says the answer is zero. The mainstream position within the three

that God desired our perfect happiness and yet created a world where none of us will attain it, which is extremely implausible. An all-good and all-powerful creator would not make perfect happiness actually unattainable for everyone by creating a world in which his purpose for human life is never realized.[31] *Mutatis mutandis*, neither would God create a world where imperfect earthly happiness is impossible or unactualized. So, we can conclude that if God exists, then both perfect happiness and imperfect happiness are possible and actual.

4.4 The Universal Desire for Perfect Happiness

A question might be raised at this juncture: Does this difference between theism and atheism really *matter*? Should we *care* about the possibility of perfect happiness? My answer is yes. This Element began with the observation that everyone wants to be happy. Now I will defend the stronger claim that everyone wants to be *perfectly* happy. We all seek a happiness that is perfect, unqualified, complete, permanent, pure, and self-sufficient.

There are a priori arguments for this thesis. Aquinas thinks it is a conceptual truth: "For the general notion of happiness consists in the perfect good ... But since good is the object of the will, the perfect good of a man is that which entirely satisfies his will. Consequently, to desire happiness is nothing else than to desire that one's will be satisfied. And this everyone desires" (1920: I-II, q. 5, a. 8). Stuart Goetz offers another conceptual argument for the proposition that all human beings desire perfect happiness:

> the idea that one might desire either a perfect happiness that is limited in duration or an unending but imperfect happiness for its own sake is conceptually suspect, if not incoherent. Because desire is conceptually ultimately aimed at both the experience of what is intrinsically good and the avoidance of what is intrinsically evil, no person can either desire the cessation of perfect happiness or prefer the experience of an imperfect happiness over that which is perfect for its own sake. (2012: 40)

In a similar vein, Jerry Walls argues:

> The fact that we seek happiness is axiomatic, but I want to sharpen this claim and insist that true happiness is by definition perfect or complete. Clearly, if some partial experience of happiness is desirable, perfect happiness is even

---

major monotheisms is that some human beings will end up in heaven and some will not. But a minority position says that all human beings ultimately will experience heavenly union with God. This debate need not concern us here because all that is needed for my argument is the much less controversial claim that at least some human beings will be perfectly happy.

[31] Anselm gives a similar argument in *Monologion* (2007a: Ch. 68–70), to the effect that if God exists then heaven (i.e., perfect happiness) must exist. For an explication and defense of this argument, see Rogers (2017).

more so. Either we have such happiness or we do not. If we do not, then it is something we want, and if we never get it, our lives will end in some degree of frustration. On the other hand, if we have it, we would not want it to end. If it did, then again, our lives would end in frustration. The only alternative to a frustrating end to our lives is perfect happiness, happiness without an end. (2002: 195)

These arguments give us some reason to think that all human beings desire perfect happiness. The potential drawback is that they rely on abstract claims about the concept of happiness and the nature of desire, which may or may not resonate with the intuitions and experiences of all individuals.

There are also a posteriori arguments for the thesis. The most widespread and significant empirical evidence comes from reflecting on the facts of human experience. The basic idea is that only perfect happiness will satisfy the deepest desires of the human heart. In support of this position, we have the testimony of humanity throughout the ages, across a wide variety of different times, places, cultures, and traditions.

One place it is apparent is in the world's great literature. Homer, Virgil, Dante, Chaucer, Shakespeare, Milton, Bunyan, Dostoyevsky, Dickinson, Eliot, O'Connor, Tolkien, and Hopkins – to name only a few – give magnificent artistic expression to the desire for perfect happiness through narrative and poetry. It is also reflected in religious and philosophical writings. The Old Testament proclaims that God has "set eternity in the human heart" (Eccles. 3:11), and Augustine says that "our hearts are restless till they rest in [God]" (2006: Bk. I, Ch. 1). Pascal's way of putting it is that "Man transcends man" (1995: No. 131). The common thread is that human happiness surpasses the human domain. We are made for something beyond ourselves, and our nature stretches out toward this transcendent goal.

Pascal, like Aquinas, says that human beings have a desire for "universal good," and "this desire is natural to man, since all men inevitably feel it, and man cannot be without it" (1995: No. 148). He argues:

A test which has gone on so long, without pause or change, really ought to convince us that we are incapable of attaining the good by our own efforts . . . . What else does this craving [for happiness], and this helplessness, proclaim but that there was once in man a true happiness, of which all that now remains is the empty print and trace. This he tries in vain to fill with everything around him, seeking in things that are not there the help he cannot find in those that are, though none can help, since the infinite abyss can be filled only with an infinite and immutable object; in other words by God himself. (1995: No. 148)

Many people, some of them far outside the Judeo-Christian orbit, seem to confirm the results of Pascal's test. Albert Camus and Jean Paul Sartre, the most well-known atheistic existentialists, recognize the desire for perfect happiness as an aspect of the human condition (see Lauinger 2012: Ch. 7). And Bertrand Russell, a nonbelieving analytic philosopher, admits in one of his personal letters: "The centre of me is always and eternally a terrible pain – a curious wild pain – a searching for something beyond what the world contains, something transfigured and infinite – the beatific vision – God" (Quoted in Kahane 2018: 95).

The desire for perfect happiness is evident in music as well. This is not limited to hymns and sacred music; it also applies to secular music. The Rolling Stones and U2 speak on behalf of humanity when they sing, respectively, "I can't get no satisfaction" and "I still haven't found what I'm looking for." The Who, another classic rock band, expresses it in their song "The Seeker": "They call me the seeker. I've been searching low and high. I won't get to get what I'm after till the day I die." The lyrics of the popular song "Shallow" from the film *A Star Is Born* express the same desire for a happiness that cannot be found in this life:

> Tell me something, girl
> Are you happy in this modern world?
> Or do you need more?
> Is there something else you're searching for?
> I'm falling
> In all the good times, I find myself longing
> for change
> And in the bad times, I fear myself.
>
> Tell me something, boy
> Aren't you tired trying to fill that void? . . .
> I'm falling
> In all the good times, I find myself longing
> for change.
> (Lady Gaga *et al.* 2018)

The testimony of humanity speaks to the *infinite* and *transcendent* character of desire: the desire for an unlimited and unreachable good, a yearning for something that no earthly good can provide. C.S. Lewis, a keen analyst of human nature, argues that all human beings have a desire for perfect heavenly happiness, even if we think we don't. He writes:

> when the real want for Heaven is present in us, we do not recognise it. Most
> people, if they had really learned to look into their own hearts, would know
> that they do want, and want acutely, something that cannot be had in this
> world. There are all sorts of things in this world that offer to give it to you, but
> they never quite keep their promise. The longings which arise in us when we
> first fall in love, or first think of some foreign country, or first take up some

subject that excites us, are longings which no marriage, no travel, no learning, can really satisfy. I am not now speaking of what would be ordinarily called unsuccessful marriages, or holidays, or learned careers. I am speaking of the best possible ones. There was something we grasped at, in that first moment of longing, which just fades away in the reality. (2002a: 112–113)

[It is] something which you were born desiring, and which, beneath the flux of other desires and in all the momentary silences between the louder passions, night and day, year by year, from childhood to old age, you are looking for, watching for, listening for[.] You have never *had* it. All the things that have ever deeply possessed your soul have been but hints of it – tantalising glimpses, promises never quite fulfilled, echoes that died away just as they caught your ear. But if it should really become manifest – if there ever came an echo that did not die away but swelled into the sound itself – you would know it. Beyond all possibility of doubt you would say "Here at last is the thing I was made for." (2002b: 639–640)

Lewis points out that the desire for God and perfect happiness is not always transparent to us. We can be unaware of it, mistake it for something else, deny it, or put it out of mind. It is "the secret signature of each soul," "the inconsolable secret in each one of [us]," "the incommunicable and unappeasable want" that is impossible to express adequately to another person (2002b: 639–640).

Lewis sometimes speaks of the longing for heaven as a "desire for our own far-off country" (1949: 4). In referring to a home that all of us are seeking, which is at the same time both familiar and foreign, he identifies one of the ways that the desire for perfect happiness can manifest itself. The same message can be heard in the hauntingly beautiful Irish ballad "The Isle of Innisfree." On the surface, the song is about the desire of an Irishman living abroad to return his native land. It begins with the following verses:

> I've met some folks who say that I'm a dreamer
> And I've no doubt there's truth in what they say
> But sure a body's bound to be a dreamer
> When all the things he loves are far away.

> And precious things are dreams unto an exile
> They take him o'er the land across the sea
> Especially when it happens he's an exile
> From that dear lovely Isle of Innisfree.

The singer then states that no other place is able to quell his yearning for home:

> And when the moonlight peeps across the rooftops
> Of this great city wondrous tho' it be
> I scarcely feel its wonder or its laughter
> I'm once again back home in Innisfree.

After dreaming of home and finding "a peace no other land could know," the song ends:

> But dreams don't last
> Tho' dreams are not forgotten
> And soon I'm back to stern reality
> But tho' they paved the footways here with gold dust
> I still would choose the Isle of Innisfree.
> (Farrelly 1950)

On one level this song is about Ireland, but on a deeper level it is about heaven. It communicates Lewis's "desire for our own far-off country," the longing for a home that is not of this world, and that we would prefer over even the happiest of earthly homes. The song can even stir that longing in the listener.

Contemporary philosophers have defended the same thesis about the infinite and transcendent character of human desire.[32] John Cottingham, for one, maintains that it is natural to human beings to have "transcendental" urges for perfect happiness, and they must be taken seriously by anyone seeking to understand human nature:

> We may want there to be an ultimate answer that stills our human restlessness, but such an answer may simply not be available. We may want there to be an ultimate source of being and goodness, but there may not be one. Nevertheless, we may at least be prepared to agree with Aquinas that "transcendent" longings in one form or another do seem to be "natural" – they are a widespread feature of human experience. So without begging any questions about their object, one may at least conclude that they merit serious attention from any philosopher interested in understanding the human condition. (2012: 235)

Cottingham rightly notes that explaining away these desires – for example, as merely the product of social conditioning, wish fulfillment, or evolutionary history – will not work because it does not do justice to human experience: "To attempt to psychologize or subjectivize all our human longings would in many cases do violence to the phenomenology involved" (2012: 243).

I will offer another argument for the claim that we all desire perfect happiness, which appeals to specific goods and features of human life. With respect to the goods that contribute to happiness, it is natural for us to want more than we can have. "More" means greater in quantity, quality, and permanence. Consider the following examples:

---

[32] See, for example, Lauinger (2012: Ch. 7). These defenses are often part of an "argument from desire" for the existence of God. That is not the sort of argument I am making here, because in this Element I am presupposing theism rather than attempting to prove it.

(1) Knowledge: We want to know more than we are capable of knowing, whether it is due to the limitations of our human minds, intelligence, time, or resources. We crave better and purer knowledge: deeper understanding, more certainty and less doubt, less confusion and error, and so on. We also want more abiding knowledge: to remember everything we learn and retain all of our precious memories instead of forgetting things over time.

(2) Friendship: We want to be friends with more people than we are capable of befriending, whether it is maintaining old friendships or making new ones, due to the limitations of time, distance, energy, state of life, and so forth. We want our relationships to be better, deeper, more loving, and more intimate, which is hindered by our natural limitations and our moral shortcomings. We want them to last when many of them do not, whether it is due to loved ones dying or friendships dissolving.

(3) Virtue: We want to be morally better, the best and ideal version of ourselves. We want to do the right thing all the time, possess all the virtues, have a clear conscience, overcome temptation, and be moral exemplars. But all of us fall short of perfect virtue. We succumb to moral weakness, make the wrong choices, harbor vices, and fail to do and be what we ought.

A similar story can be told about the other elements of happiness. The yearning for more goodness is a natural one that we can all discover through our experience of imperfect goods. It shows that the best we can achieve in earthly life is imperfect happiness, and that we have a desire for perfect happiness that cannot be satisfied by any created good.

The empirical argument in this section has appealed to claims about human nature, desire, and experience that are meant to apply to all human beings. For this reason, it is worth repeating a point from Section 3 about the two general kinds of evidence that are relevant to these sorts of claims: arguments and experiences. The latter looms large for the questions we have covered in this section. It is not the only source of reasons, but for some people it may be more accessible and compelling, and these questions will be easier to answer through reflective introspection and lived experience than through philosophical analysis and argument. At the end of the day, each of us has to consider these claims in light of our own life to see if they ring true. Perhaps the best we can do is attend to our experience carefully, reflect on it honestly, and share it with others to see if it aligns with theirs. This can be challenging, especially when dealing with something as personal, mysterious, and psychologically complex as our deepest desires. There is undoubtedly some truth in the biblical adage that "The heart is deceitful above all things, and desperately corrupt; who can understand it?" (Jer. 17:9). In the end, I can only appeal to the readers to consider their own experience – as well as the philosophical arguments – as carefully and honestly as they can.

4.5 The Uniqueness of Theism

I have argued that if God exists, then perfect happiness is possible (and actual). Now, to end this section, I will defend the stronger claim that theism *alone* allows for perfect happiness: perfect happiness is possible (and, by extension, actual) *if and only if* God exists. As Aquinas puts it, "man is made happy by God alone" (1920: I-II, q. 5, a. 6).

Applying the criteria for perfect happiness identified in Subsection 4.1, the contention is that union with God is the only way to experience a happiness that is unqualified, complete, permanent, pure, and self-sufficient. I will focus on completeness and self-sufficiency. Section 3 showed that God, in virtue of being the source and paradigm of all value, brings maximal happiness to human beings, regardless of how one understands the nature and content of happiness. All types of goodness, both objective and subjective, originate from God and are realized in their highest form when a human person is united with God. God alone is essentially goodness itself, the most perfect and complete goodness there is.

The arguments in Subsections 4.2 and 4.4 establish that some of our desires cannot be fully satisfied in this life due to the finitude and the flaws of our earthly existence. Only union with God can fulfill the deepest longings of the human heart. God not only satisfies all of our desires in the quantitative sense that we have no unfulfilled desires, but also in the qualitative sense that our desires are fulfilled in the most complete and deepest way possible (which cannot happen in this life). God alone is *infinitely* and *perfectly* good, which is why God alone can satisfy our desires both quantitatively and qualitatively. Couched in terms of the three "transcendental" desires for truth, goodness, and beauty, we can say that human beings desire these three things in their unlimited and best possible form. Only God, whose nature is identical to truth, goodness, and beauty themselves, can fulfill these fundamental human desires. Assuming that these transcendental goods have objective value as well, only in God can they be found in their most valuable form.

The objection might be raised that there are other worldviews that can secure perfect happiness, not just theism. The most promising candidate is probably Platonism. According to one interpretation of Plato's metaphysics, the human soul is immortal, virtuous individuals will have a good afterlife, and it will consist in perfect knowledge of the Forms – non-spatiotemporal abstract objects that are the ideal essences of things – especially the Forms of Truth, Goodness, and Beauty. Like God, these three Platonic Forms are the eternal, infinite, and perfect instances of the three transcendentals. Thus, the objection goes, human persons in the afterlife can experience perfect happiness because their desires for truth, goodness, and beauty will be satisfied by knowledge of the Forms and contact with these abstract objective values. A human person in this state can experience a happiness that is unqualified, complete, permanent, pure, and self-sufficient.

In response to this objection, I maintain that Platonism is inferior to theism with respect to securing human happiness. The main reason is that Platonic Forms are impersonal beings whereas God is a personal being. You cannot have a personal relationship with an abstract universal Form, but you can have one with the concrete individual who is God. Having a personal relationship with the absolute locus of truth, goodness, and beauty is better than not having one; the interpersonal union between a human person and a divine person adds something of great intrinsic value. It also satisfies a deep desire that we have. The infinite and transcendental desires that we have discussed in this section involve a desire for not just any sort of contact with truth, goodness, and beauty, but a desire to be *united* with them, to *commune* with them, to be *at one* with them. Lewis makes this point regarding beauty:

> What more, you may ask, do we want? Ah, but we want so much more – something the books on aesthetics take little notice of. But the poets and the mythologies know all about it. We do not want merely to *see* beauty, though, God knows, even that is bounty enough. We want something else which can hardly be put into words – to be united with the beauty we see, to pass into it, to receive it into ourselves, to bathe in it, to become part of it. (1949: 12–13)

Ironically, Plato himself appears to agree. When describing the supreme happiness of contemplating the Forms, he often uses relational language such as the following: "if [someone] could see the divine Beauty itself in its one form ... Do you think it would be a poor life for a human being to look there and to *behold* it by that which he ought, and to *be with* it? ... because he is *in touch with* the true Beauty" (1997: 211e–212a, emphasis added). What goes for beauty also goes for truth and goodness. On a theistic perspective, this longing is equivalent to a desire for union with the God who is beauty, truth, and goodness.

A relational and interpersonal union between a human person and a divine person is more objectively valuable and more subjectively satisfying than a purely intellectual and impersonal union between a human mind and a Platonic Form. Because human beings are by nature persons, our happiness and fulfillment must engage our personal and social nature. If we did not have such a relationship with a personal God, an aspect of ourselves would be unfulfilled and a desire of ours would be unsatisfied, which means we would not be perfectly happy. For this reason, theism can secure perfect happiness but Platonism cannot. A similar problem will apply to all non-theistic worldviews. Even if they could allow for a happiness that is pure and permanent, it cannot be complete and self-sufficient. Even if they could overcome one of the obstacles to perfect happiness – the presence of evil – by, say, affirming that human beings are immortal and will experience an afterlife containing no vice, suffering, or death – they cannot match theism with respect to the other obstacle – the absence of good – which comes only through an interpersonal union with an infinitely and perfectly good divine person.[33]

In closing, we can return to Augustine's theme of the "restless heart," which is another expression of the view that perfect happiness is found in God alone. The universal desire for happiness is at bottom a desire for God, and the human heart will find rest only in an unending relationship of loving union with the personal God, and with other human persons who share in it. Those who experience this heavenly union will be able to say, with Augustine and with Sydney Carton, the hero of Dickens's *A Tale of Two Cities*, "It is a far, far better thing that I do, than I have ever done; it is a far, far better rest that I go to than I have ever known" (2014: 451).

4.6 Conclusion

This section has investigated the question of whether human beings can be happy. The opposing answers that theism and atheism give to this question reveal one of the most striking differences between these worldviews. On an atheistic picture, perfect happiness is impossible, and imperfect happiness is either impossible or possible but highly precarious. On a theistic picture, by contrast, perfect and imperfect happiness are both possible. Although the imperfect happiness of earthly life is not attainable for everyone, perfect happiness in the next life is something that every human person can experience. Moreover, perfect happiness is not just a mere possibility but an actual reality. Theism therefore avoids pessimism about the prospects for happiness and affirms an optimistic view of human life. Because happiness is something we value highly and desire strongly, this is one of the most significant advantages of theism over atheism. And if it is true, as I have argued, that God alone can make

---

[33] Against the potential objection that the personal being in question need not be the monotheistic God – a single divine being who alone possesses all the standard divine attributes – the theistic tradition has held that there can be only one being who is perfectly good and whose nature is goodness itself, and that such a being necessarily will possess the other divine attributes such as omniscience, omnipotence, and eternality. The conclusion that only one divine being can possess all perfections is entailed by the two constraints on the theistic concept of God that were discussed in Section 1: God is the creator and first cause who is absolutely metaphysically ultimate, and God is the greatest conceivable being who is absolutely perfect.

us perfectly happy and satisfy the deepest desires of the human heart, this lends considerable support to the idea that, as far as happiness is concerned, a theistic world is the best and most desirable one to live in.

We have focused on the possibility of happiness considered as an *end* or *goal*. We might also wonder about the *means* or *process* by which a person becomes happy. This is a question that cannot be explored in this work, in part because space does not permit it, but also because most theists believe that the answer depends primarily on what we know by divine revelation rather than human reason, and thus falls more within the province of theology rather than philosophy. For the sake of saying something about this question, however, I will end this section with a brief summary of one (but not the only) traditional answer given by Christian theism. In short, human beings cannot attain happiness by our own efforts, but only by divine grace, that is, God's supernatural assistance. We need divine help in order to be made capable of union with God. In this way, happiness is a gift, not an accomplishment. At the same time, whether we are happy is not up to God alone. It partly depends on us and is within our control. God gives everyone the opportunity to enter into loving union with him, but each individual has the free choice to accept or reject God's offer, and therefore to be happy or unhappy. The process by which a human person comes into union with God consists of God making the first move and extending his offer of friendship, and a human person responding by freely knowing and loving God in return (for further study, see Aquinas 1920: I-II, q. 5, a. 5–6; Walls 2002: Ch. 3; Stump 2010: Ch. 5–8). This is one theistic answer to the question of how to be truly happy.

5 The Hope of Happiness

5.1 The Axiology of Theism

At the beginning of this Element, I said that one of the ways to evaluate worldviews is to consider their implications for the things we care about. One of these things is happiness, for we all believe that happiness matters and we all want to be happy. So, when evaluating theism as a worldview, what God means for happiness should be an important consideration.

I have argued that theism has significant theoretical and practical implications for human happiness. On the theoretical side, theism supplies answers to some of the biggest philosophical questions we can ask about happiness, including its nature, content, structure, and possibility. It implies that there are objective truths about happiness that apply to all human beings. It provides a pluralistic model of the nature and content of happiness that can accommodate many of our leading philosophical theories and commonsense intuitions while giving them a deeper foundation in God. It implies that there is a hierarchy of value with union with God as the supreme good. It shows that the horizon of happiness extends beyond earthly life and includes the afterlife. And it tells us that God wants us to be perfectly happy.

On the practical side, theism says that perfect happiness is possible for every human being. The universal desire for perfect happiness is not in vain but can be fulfilled. Thus, it is rational to act for the goal of perfect happiness in heaven. Theism also implies that happiness is both a gift that everyone is offered and something that is up to us. It is partly in our control and partly out of our control, which is better than the alternatives of it being totally beyond our control, robbing us of agency and leaving us powerless with respect to our happiness, or totally dependent on us, which leads to despair because no one is capable of attaining perfect happiness by one's own efforts. Finally, theism says that the source of true happiness and the greatest good for every person is knowing and loving God. This means that everyone has a reason to pursue union with God and to incorporate it into one's life plan, and indeed to prioritize it as the most important good for oneself and for others.

Taken together, all of these implications amount to a strong reason to give theism serious consideration (or reconsideration) as a worldview. They are also relevant to the "axiology of theism" debate. Recall that this dispute is about whether God's existence is (or would be) a good thing. Pro-theism answers yes, while anti-theism answers no. This Element contains a pro-theism argument by identifying a significant axiological strength of theism. The theistic picture of happiness is a positive, optimistic, and desirable one. If God exists, we are capable of a happiness that is better in every way than the happiness we could have if God did not exist. Perfect happiness, which is impossible in an atheistic world, is a real possibility for us. This is a major advantage of theism.

To be more precise, I have defended an argument for "narrow" pro-theism that focuses solely on the value of happiness and contends that *with respect to human happiness*, it is better if God exists than if God does not exist. I have not offered an argument for "wide" pro-theism to the effect that theism is superior to atheism *overall* and *all things considered,* taking all the relevant values into account. With that said, my argument does not just support the narrow conclusion that there is *a* good that favors theism. The good in question – perfect happiness in union with God – is the *highest good possible* for human beings. Its value is greater than all (or nearly all) the other benefits usually put forward to support either anti-theism or theism, such as privacy, autonomy, subjective meaning in life, cosmic justice, immortality, and the defeat of suffering. Establishing wide pro-theism would require comparing all the various good and evils on theism and on atheism to determine which worldview on balance has a greater proportion of goods to evils and therefore is best overall. I will not do that here. But the fact that union with God is the greatest good for human beings considerably strengthens the case for wide pro-theism. What magnifies the point is that happiness is a larger and more inclusive good than the more specific goods typically discussed in the literature, because it encompasses *anything and everything* that is good for human persons. This makes its axiological weight much greater, and the case for wide pro-theism much stronger.

In addition, my argument can overcome what is perhaps the strongest objection to pro-theism arguments: the objection that theistic goods do not really require God. Guy Kahane, for one, argues that all or most of the goods that are alleged benefits of theism are not unique to theism and can obtain without God. Thus, they do not support the pro-theism position. As Kahane summarizes it,

> while the benefits mentioned in [theistic worlds] are expected *upshots* of God's existence, *they do not inherently require God's existence* .... [Y]ou can't have God without the negative stuff, but you *can* have the positive stuff *without* God – and thus without the negative stuff. So the best possible worlds are ones in which we still enjoy the benefits of a Godly world but where God doesn't exist. (2018: 102)

For instance, perhaps a quasi-divine being who is very knowledgeable, powerful, and good, but who falls short of possessing the divine omni-attributes, can still secure benefits like immortality, cosmic justice, and the defeat of suffering. Kahane goes so far as to claim that "Even heaven and hell (if one wants to tie [the two theistic benefits of] immortality and cosmic justice in this way), could run just fine without a divine overlord" (2018: 102).

This objection has no force against the happiness argument for pro-theism. As I have argued, heavenly union with God is the *best* possible happiness and the *only* possible *perfect* happiness. The goodness of knowing and loving God perfectly and everlastingly is something that can obtain only on theism. God is the sole and unique absolutely perfect and metaphysically ultimate being, and God alone is infinite and perfect goodness, truth, and beauty. Nothing less can bring us the perfect happiness we seek, so nothing other than God will do. In short, perfect heavenly happiness is a significant good that requires God. Kahane's assertion that heaven is possible without God is simply confused, because heaven essentially just is union with God.

Finally, the considerations explored in this Element can help to rebut one of the central arguments for the opposing "anti-theist" position that God's existence is (or would be) a bad thing. In a frequently cited passage, Thomas Nagel confesses, "I hope there is no God! I don't want there to be a God; I don't want the universe to be like that" (1997: 130). Kahane and other anti-theists try to justify Nagel's attitude by arguing that "God's existence is logically incompatible with the full realization of certain values," such as privacy, autonomy, and subjective meaning, and "His existence places an upper limit on their realization" (Kahane 2011: 682–683). The exact opposite is true with respect to happiness. It is atheism, not theism, that places a limit on the kind and degree of happiness that is available to us. As I have argued, theism alone is compatible with the full realization of human happiness – one of the most important values in life – because perfect happiness can be had only through everlasting union with God. When it comes to happiness, the theist can say to the secular philosopher: "There are more things in heaven and on earth than are dreamt of in your philosophy." For this reason, contrary to the attitude expressed by Nagel, we *should want* to live in a theistic world. Since desire aims at the good, we should want God to exist because it would be a good thing for us. More precisely, insofar as happiness is concerned, we should want God to exist because it would be the best thing for our happiness, which is something we all desire. We should also *hope* there is a God. The nature of this hope will be the final topic we explore.[34]

5.2 Hope

The term "hope" can pick out different things. We will briefly examine three senses of hope and their connection to happiness. The first is *propositional hope*: hope *that* some outcome occurs. According to the standard account, hope is distinct from other propositional attitudes like belief and desire. It is a compound attitude with a cognitive component and a conative component: S hopes that $p = S$ believes that p is possible and S desires p (Bloeser and Stahl 2022).[35] The belief condition specifies that we hope for things we consider to be possible. We cannot think the outcome in question is either impossible or certain; but it need not be probable because we can hope for things that we take to be possible but unlikely. The desire condition specifies that we hope for things we consider good or desirable. Regarding the rationality of hope, there is somewhat of a consensus among philosophers that S's hope that p is epistemically rational if p is possible and S is justified in believing that p is possible; and

---

[34] These considerations might also support the position that it is practically rational *overall* to desire and act as though God exists, and/or pragmatically rational to *believe* that God exists. It would take more argument to establish these further conclusions, however.

[35] This standard definition of hope is disputed, with some arguing that it needs to be supplemented with one or more additional conditions, such as an affective component, and others arguing that hope is irreducible to belief and desire and constitutes a sui generis mental state.

practically rational if *S*'s hope that *p* is instrumentally valuable for the promotion of *S*'s ends (Bloeser and Stahl 2022).

On a theistic worldview, it is rational to hope for happiness, including perfect happiness. If theism is true, then happiness is an end that is both possible and desirable for all human persons. It is also something that can be attained only with God's help. And it is an end that God, in his goodness and love, offers to all human beings. If theism is true, then we can and should hope *that* we will be perfectly happy in the future, and hope *in* God to make it so.

The second meaning of hope is hope as an *emotion* or *passion*. According to contemporary philosopher Robert C. Roberts, hope is an emotion marked by "a construal of one's future as holding good prospects" (2007: 148). On Aquinas's older account of hope as a passion, hope concerns both an end and a means. As an end, it aims at some good; as a means, it concerns the way we achieve the good. Aquinas explains:

> Hope can regard two things. For it regards as its object, the good which one hopes for. But since the good we hope for is something difficult but possible to obtain; and since it happens sometimes that what is difficult becomes possible to us, not through ourselves but through others; hence it is that hope regards also that by which something becomes possible to us. (1920: I-II, q. 40, a. 7)

Aquinas gives a more specific analysis on which the object of hope must be something that is good, in the future, possible, and difficult to achieve (1920: I-II, q. 40, a. 1). The theistic conception of hope satisfies all four of Aquinas's conditions, as well as Roberts's shorter definition. Hope is an emotion that is natural, appropriate, and conducive to human flourishing. God has designed our affective nature so that hope inclines us toward the happiness for which we were created.

Third, hope can be considered as a *virtue* or good state of character. It was Christianity that first made hope a virtue, and it has been understood as a "theological virtue" with essentially theistic components. In the Christian tradition, hope is a supernatural virtue of the will that directs us to God and is infused by divine grace. Aquinas's account of the virtue of hope builds on his analysis of hope as a passion with some key modifications. Whereas the object of ordinary hope is future happiness understood in terms of finite and imperfect earthly goods, the object of virtuous hope is the highest good of perfect happiness in heaven. It involves a desire for everlasting happiness with God, and it is the virtue by which "the will is directed to this end ... as something attainable" (1920: I-II, q. 62, a. 3). The virtue of hope concerns both happiness (the end) and God's gracious help in attaining it (the means). It is the virtue by which "we trust to the divine assistance for obtaining happiness" (1920: I-II, q. 17, a. 6).

Putting this together, we can define virtuous hope as desiring to attain perfect happiness and believing and trusting that God will help us to reach it. By hope, we keep our "eyes on the prize" and continue striving for heaven as our ultimate goal, and we rely on God's help in getting us there. We can also think of it as a settled disposition to believe and feel that in the end, thanks to God, "all shall be well, and all shall be well, and all manner of thing shall be well," as Julian of Norwich says (1966: 103–104). If theism is true, then hope is a real virtue because the object of hope – perfect happiness – is something we can, with God's help, attain. This brings us to one last difference between the theistic and atheistic worldviews.

5.3 Theistic versus Atheistic Hope

In the *Critique of Pure Reason*, Kant famously says that one of the three central questions of philosophy is "What may I hope?" As he recognizes, the answer to this question depends on one's religious beliefs, and theists and atheists give (or should give) radically different answers. For the atheist Schopenhauer, any hope for happiness is a false hope, and the only reasonable attitude is despair:

> Life presents itself as a continual deception in small things as in great. If it has promised, it does not keep its word, unless to show how little worth desiring were the things desired: thus we are deluded now by hope, now by what was hoped for. If it has given, it did so in order to take … Life with its hourly, daily, weekly, yearly, little, greater, and great misfortunes, with its deluded hopes and its accidents destroying all our calculations, bears so distinctly the impression of something with which we must become disgusted, that it is hard to conceive how one has been able to mistake this and allow oneself to be persuaded that life is there in order to be thankfully enjoyed, and that man exists in order to be happy. (2008: 114–115)

Bertrand Russell's outlook is not as bleak, but he still acknowledges that perfect happiness is impossible in an atheistic universe. He recommends resignation: lowering our concern for happiness, desiring it less, and reducing our efforts to achieve it. According to Russell, we should "abandon the struggle for private happiness" while preserving "our respect for truth, for beauty, for the ideal of perfection which life does not permit us to attain," accepting the fact that "to every man comes, sooner or later, the great renunciation" (1999: 37, 34, 35).

The outlooks of both thinkers are ultimately forms of despair, which is the antithesis of hope. The reason is that they both take perfect happiness to be impossible and counsel us to give up on ever reaching this end that we all desire. Schopenhauer recommends outright despondency and hopelessness, and Russell's resignation is really a form of despair underneath the mask of "putting on a happy face." With admirable honesty, he admits as much in his popular essay "A Free Man's Worship," when he says that human beings can stand "only on the firm foundation of unyielding despair" (1999: 32).

The reflections of clear-eyed atheists like these reveal that hope in the traditional and fullest sense (encompassing propositional, emotional, and virtuous hope) does not make sense on atheism and is intelligible only on theism (for further discussion, see Cottingham 2009: 154–157). On the theistic view, it is reasonable to believe in, desire, and pursue perfect happiness, and to cultivate the attitude, emotion, and virtue of hope. We can strive for happiness without falling into despair about the possibility of achieving it, maintaining the hope of heavenly happiness with the assistance of a loving and provident God. Theists can agree with the sentiment expressed by the character Andy Dufresne at the end of the film *The Shawshank Redemption:* "Hope is a good thing, maybe the best of things. And no good thing ever dies." In contrast to Schopenhauer's forlornness and Russell's resignation, the right attitude toward future happiness is the one the aged Odysseus has toward future journeys and glorious adventures:

> For always roaming with a hungry heart . . . .
> And this gray spirit yearning in desire
> To follow knowledge like a sinking star,
> Beyond the utmost bound of human thought . . . .
> . . . my purpose holds
> To sail beyond the sunset, and the baths
> Of all the western stars, until I die . . . .
> Made weak by time and fate, but strong in will
> To strive, to seek, to find, and not to yield.
> (Tennyson 1908: 26–29)

5.4 Conclusion

To end this Element, we can return to the place where it began: Plato's adage that philosophy begins in wonder. One of the things we wonder about and care deeply about is happiness, which is why it is a perennial topic of philosophical reflection. Theism has much to say about human happiness. It provides theoretical answers to some of our most fundamental questions and practical solutions to our lifelong quest for happiness. Its "good news" about happiness is one of the most salient and attractive features of the theistic worldview. If God exists, then the reason why everyone wants to be happy is that God created us for happiness.

When discussing why people today should consider believing in God and making a commitment to a religious way of life, John Cottingham highlights the fact that theism allows for an alignment between the nature of reality and our deepest desires for the values of truth, goodness, and beauty. He writes:

[O]ne is struck by the extent to which religious belief offers a *home* for our aspirations. Theism, in its traditional form found in the three great Abrahamic faiths, involves the idea of a *match* between our aspirations and our ultimate destiny. On this picture, the creative power that ultimately shaped us is itself the source of the values we find ourselves constrained to acknowledge, and has made our nature such that we can find true fulfilment only in seeking those values. (2009: 5)

Theism speaks to the deepest longings of the human heart and claims to be able to fulfill them. It tells us that we can hope for a happiness in the next life that is far superior to even the best happiness we can experience in this life. It says that we are made for everlasting perfect happiness in union with an infinitely good and loving God, and that God wills this for us and is willing to offer it to us as a gift to be received. If that isn't worth wondering about, what is?

References

Adams, Robert M. (1999). *Finite and Infinite Goods: A Framework for Ethics*, Oxford: Oxford University Press.

Alighieri, Dante (2008). *Paradiso*, R. Hollander and J. Hollander, trans., New York: Anchor Books.

Annas, Julia (1993). *The Morality of Happiness*, New York: Oxford University Press.

Annas, Julia (2004). Happiness as Achievement. *Daedalus*, 133(2), 44–51.

Anselm (2007a). *Monologion*. In T. Williams, trans. and ed., *Anselm: Basic Writings*, Indianapolis: Hackett, 1–73.

Anselm (2007b). *On the Fall of the Devil*. In T. Williams, trans. and ed., *Anselm: Basic Writings*, Indianapolis: Hackett, 167–212.

Anselm (2007c). *Proslogion*. In T. Williams, trans. and ed., *Anselm: Basic Writings*, Indianapolis: Hackett, 75–98.

Aquinas, Thomas (1920). *Summa Theologiae*, Fathers of the English Dominican Province, trans., London: Burns, Oates & Washbourne.

Aquinas, Thomas (1955). *Summa Contra Gentiles*, A.C. Pegis, J.F. Anderson, V.J. Bourke, and C.J. O'Neil, trans., New York: Hanover House.

Aristotle (1984). *Nicomachean Ethics*, W.D. Ross, trans. In J. Barnes, ed., *The Complete Works of Aristotle: The Revised Oxford Translation*, Vol. 2, Princeton: Princeton University Press, 1729–1867.

Augustine (1887a). *De Trinitate*, A.W. Haddan, trans. In P. Schaff, ed., *Nicene and Post-Nicene Fathers*, Vol. 3, Buffalo: Christian Literature. www.newadvent.org/fathers/1301.htm, 1–228.

Augustine (1887b). *On the Morals of the Catholic Church*, R. Stothert, trans. In P. Schaff, ed., *Nicene and Post-Nicene Fathers*, Vol. 4, Buffalo: Christian Literature. www.newadvent.org/fathers/1401.htm, 37–64.

Augustine (2006). *Confessions*, 2nd ed., F.J. Sheed, trans., Indianapolis: Hackett.

Augustine (2012). *The City of God*, 2 Vols., W. Babcock, trans., Hyde Park: New City Press.

Baril, Anne (2016). Virtue and Well-Being. In G. Fletcher, ed., *The Routledge Handbook of Philosophy of Well-Being*, London: Routledge, 242–258.

Barrington-Leigh, Christopher P. (2022). Trends in Conceptions of Progress and Well-Being. In J.F. Helliwell, R. Layard, J.D. Sachs et al., eds., *World Happiness Report 2022*, New York: Sustainable Development Solutions Network, 53–74.

Bloeser, Claudia, and Titus Stahl (2022). Hope. In E.N. Zalta, ed., *The Stanford Encyclopedia of Philosophy*, summer ed. https://plato.stanford.edu/archives/sum2022/entries/hope/.

Boethius (2001). *Consolation of Philosophy*, J.C. Relihan, trans., Indianapolis: Hackett.

Budziszewski, J. (2020). *Commentary on Thomas Aquinas's Treatise on Happiness and Ultimate Purpose*, Cambridge: Cambridge University Press.

Butler, Joseph (1983). *Five Sermons*, S.L. Darwall, ed., Indianapolis: Hackett.

Calvin, John (1845). *Institutes of the Christian Religion*, H. Beveridge, trans., Grand Rapids: Christian Classics Ethereal Library. https://ccel.org/ccel/calvin/institutes/institutes.

Carson, Thomas L. (2000). *Value and the Good Life*, Notre Dame: University of Notre Dame Press.

Catholic Church (1995). *Catechism of the Catholic Church*, 2nd ed., New York: Doubleday.

Cicero (1931). *De Finibus Bonorum et Malorum*, H. Rackham, trans., London: William Heinemann. https://archive.org/details/definibusbonorum00cice/page/n5/mode/2up?ref=ol&view=theater].

Cottingham, John (2009). *Why Believe?* London: Continuum.

Cottingham, John (2012). Human Nature and the Transcendent. *Royal Institute of Philosophy Supplement*, 70, 233–254.

Crisp, Roger (2006). *Reasons and the Good*, Oxford: Clarendon Press.

Davies, Brian (2021). *An Introduction to the Philosophy of Religion*, 4th ed., New York: Oxford University Press.

Dickens, Charles (2014). *A Tale of Two Cities*, Minneapolis: Lerner.

Edwards, Jonathan (1746). *Religions Affections*, Grand Rapids: Christian Classics Ethereal Library. https://ccel.org/ccel/e/edwards/affections.

Fagothey, Austin (1959). *Right and Reason*, 2nd ed., Charlotte: TAN Books.

Farrelly, Dick (1950). *The Isle of Innisfree*, London: Peter Maurice Music.

Feldman, Fred (2004). *Pleasure and the Good Life: Concerning the Nature, Varieties, and Plausibility of Hedonism*, Oxford: Clarendon Press.

Finnis, John (2011). *Natural Law and Natural Rights*, 2nd ed., Oxford: Oxford University Press.

Fletcher, Guy (2016). *The Philosophy of Well-Being: An Introduction*, London: Routledge.

Garcia, Laura (2008). Moral Perfection. In T.P. Flint and M.C. Rea, eds., *The Oxford Handbook of Philosophical Theology*, Oxford: Oxford University Press, 217–238.

Goetz, Stewart (2012). *The Purpose of Life: A Theistic Perspective*, London: Continuum.

Haybron, Daniel (2013). *Happiness: A Very Short Introduction*, Oxford: Oxford University Press.

Heathwood, Chris (2021). *Happiness and Well-Being*, Cambridge: Cambridge University Press

Helliwell, John F., Richard Layard, and Jeffrey Sachs, eds. (2012). *World Happiness Report 2012*, New York: UN Sustainable Development Solutions Network.

Herbert, George (2016). *100 Poems*, H. Wilcox, ed., Cambridge: Cambridge University Press.

Hooker, Brad (2015). The Elements of Well-Being. *Journal of Practical Ethics*, 3(1), 15–35.

Hudson, Hud (2021). *Fallenness and Flourishing*, Oxford: Oxford University Press.

Hurka, Thomas (1993). *Perfectionism*, Oxford: Clarendon Press.

Irwin, Terence (2007). *The Development of Ethics*, 3 Vols., Oxford: Oxford University Press.

Julian of Norwich (1966). *Revelations of Divine Love*, C. Wolters, trans., London: Penguin Books.

Kaczor, Christopher (2019). *The Gospel of Happiness: How Secular Psychology Points to the Wisdom of Christian Happiness*, 2nd ed., South Bend: St. Augustine's Press.

Kahane, Guy (2011). Should We Want God to Exist? *Philosophy and Phenomenological Research*, 82(3), 674–696.

Kahane, Guy (2018). If There Is a Hole, It Is Not God-Shaped. In K.J. Kraay, ed., *Does God Matter? Essays on the Axiological Consequences of Theism*, New York: Routledge, 95–131.

Kant, Immanuel (2012). *Groundwork of the Metaphysics of Morals*, revised ed., M. Gregor and J. Timmerman, trans. and ed., Cambridge: Cambridge University Press.

Kraay, Klaas J. (2021). *The Axiology of Theism*, Cambridge: Cambridge University Press.

Kraut, Richard (2007). *What Is Good and Why: The Ethics of Well-Being*, Cambridge, MA: Harvard University Press.

Lady Gaga, Andrew Wyatt, Anthony Rossomando, and Mark Ronson (2018). *Shallow*, Los Angeles: Interscope Records.

Lauinger, William A. (2012). *Well-Being and Theism: Linking Ethics to God*, London: Continuum.

Lauinger, William A. (2016). Well-Being in the Christian Tradition. In G. Fletcher, ed., *The Routledge Handbook of Philosophy of Well-Being*, London: Routledge, 81–94.

Lewis, C. S. (1949). The Weight of Glory. In *The Weight of Glory and Other Addresses*, New York: Macmillan.

Lewis, C. S. (2002a). *Mere Christianity*. In *The Complete C.S. Lewis Signature Classics*, New York: Harper Collins, 1–177.

Lewis, C. S. (2002b). *The Problem of Pain*. In *The Complete C.S. Lewis Signature Classics*, New York: Harper Collins, 543–646.

McPherson, David (2020). *Virtue and Meaning: A Neo-Aristotelian Perspective*, Cambridge: Cambridge University Press.

Mill, Jon Stuart (2001). *Utilitarianism*, 2nd ed., G. Sher, ed., Indianapolis: Hackett.

Murphy, Mark (2001). *Natural Law and Practical Rationality*, Cambridge: Cambridge University Press.

Nagel, Thomas (1997). *The Last Word*, New York: Oxford University Press.

Pascal, Blaise (1995). *Pensées*, A.J. Krailsheimer, trans., London: Penguin Books.

Peterson, Michael, William Hasker, Bruce Reichenbauch, and David Basinger, eds. (2013). *Reason and Religious Belief: An Introduction to the Philosophy of Religion*, 5th ed., Oxford: Oxford University Press.

Plato (1956). *Symposium*, B. Jowett, trans., New York: The Liberal Arts Press.

Plato (1990). *Theaetetus*, M. J. Levett and M. Burnyeat, trans., Indianapolis: Hackett.

Plato (1997). *Symposium*, A. Nehamas and P. Woodruff, trans. In John M. Cooper, ed., *Plato: Complete Works*, Indianapolis: Hackett, 457–505.

Rice, Christopher M. (2013). Defending the Objective List Theory of Well-Being. *Ratio*, 26(2), 196–211.

Roberts, Robert C. (2007). *Spiritual Emotions: A Psychology of Christian Virtues*, Grand Rapids: Eerdmans.

Rogers, Katherin (2017). Anselmian Meditations on Heaven. In T. Ryan Byerly and Eric J. Silverman, eds., *Paradise Understood: New Philosophical Essays about Heaven*, Oxford: Oxford University Press, 30–48.

Russell, Bertrand (1930). *The Conquest of Happiness*, New York: Horace Liveright.

Russell, Bertrand (1999). The Free Man's Worship. In Louis Greenspan and Stefan Andersson, eds., *Russell on Religion*, New York: Routledge, 31–38.

Russell, Bertrand (2004). *What I Believe*, London: Routledge.

Russell, Daniel (2012). *Happiness for Humans*, Oxford: Oxford University Press.

Schopenhauer, Arthur (2008). On the Variety and Suffering of Life, R. B. Haldane and J. Kemp, trans. In Steven M. Cahn and Christine Vitrano, eds., *Happiness: Classic and Contemporary Readings in Philosophy*, Oxford: Oxford University Press, 114–121.

Seneca (2007). On the Happy Life, J. W. Basore, trans. In Steven M. Cahn and Christine Vitrano, eds., *Happiness: Classic and Contemporary Readings in Philosophy*, New York: Oxford University Press, 41–51.

Shakespeare, William (2008a). *Othello*. In S. Greenblatt, ed., *The Norton Shakespeare*, 2nd ed., New York: W.W. Norton, 2109–2191.

Shakespeare, William (2008b). *Romeo and Juliet*. In S. Greenblatt, ed., *The Norton Shakespeare*, 2nd ed., New York: W.W. Norton, 897–972.

Sobel, David (2016). *From Valuing to Value: A Defense of Subjectivism*, Oxford: Oxford University Press.

Stenberg, Joseph (2019). The All-Happy God. *Faith and Philosophy*, 36(4), 423–441.

Stump, Eleonore (2010). *Wandering in Darkness: Narrative and the Problem of Suffering*, Oxford: Oxford University Press.

Stump, Eleonore and Norman Kretzmann (1988). Being and Goodness. In Thomas V. Morris, ed, *Divine and Human Action: Essays in the Metaphysics of Theism*, Ithaca: Cornell University Press, 281–312.

Taylor, Richard (2002). *Virtue Ethics*, Amherst: Prometheus Books.

Tennyson, Alfred Lord (1908). Ulysses. In Hallam, Lord Tennyson, ed., *The Works of Tennyson*, London: Macmillan, 26–29.

Walls, Jerry L. (2002). *Heaven: The Logic of Eternal Joy*, Oxford: Oxford University Press.

Westminster Shorter Catechism. 1647. www.westminsterconfession.org/resources/confessional-standards/the-westminster-shorter-catechism/.

White, Nicholas (2006). *A Brief History of Happiness*, Malden: Blackwell.

Acknowledgments

I am very grateful to Michael Peterson and Joel Archer for the opportunity to write this Element and for their wise counsel; Duane Armitage, Christopher Hauser, James Hynds, David McPherson, Eleonore Stump, and my family for the encouragement to write it; John Crosby, Brandon Dahm, Logan Gage, Luca Gariffo, Christopher Kaczor, Richard Kim, Robert Kim-Farley, James Kintz, William Lauinger, Alex Plato, Rashad Rehman, Jeremy Skrzypek, and Paul Symington for helpful conversations and/or reading recommendations; Franciscan University for granting me a course reduction to work on the project; and my colleagues in the Philosophy Department for their support and advice. Special thanks are owed to the following individuals who read the manuscript and provided feedback on it: Aileen Casillas, Anthony Chipps, Brandon Dahm, Amedeo Da Pra Galanti, Miguel De La Torre, Logan Gage, Medhanie Ghenzebu, Francisco Guizar, Michael Hall, Jacob Hollis, Patrick Lee, Maisie Leonard, Fr. Emmanuel Nwosu, Sharon Phillips, Paul Symington, Isabel Thibodeaux, Benjamin Van Norstrand, and Andrew Zsebedics. I am very grateful to Richard Kim, Robert Kim-Farley, Rashad Rehman, and an anonymous reviewer at Cambridge University Press for reading the entire manuscript and offering detailed comments. Finally, special thanks to my wife Kathleen Shea. Without her love, support, and sacrifice, this work – and my happiness – would not have been possible.

Cambridge Elements ≡

The Problems of God

Series Editor

Michael L. Peterson
Asbury Theological Seminary

Michael L. Peterson is Professor of Philosophy at Asbury Theological Seminary. He is the author of *God and Evil* (Routledge); *Monotheism, Suffering, and Evil* (Cambridge University Press); *With All Your Mind* (University of Notre Dame Press); *C. S. Lewis and the Christian Worldview* (Oxford University Press); *Evil and the Christian God* (Baker Book House); and *Philosophy of Education: Issues and Options* (Intervarsity Press). He is co-author of *Reason and Religious Belief* (Oxford University Press); *Science, Evolution, and Religion: A Debate about Atheism and Theism* (Oxford University Press); and *Biology, Religion, and Philosophy* (Cambridge University Press). He is editor of *The Problem of Evil: Selected Readings* (University of Notre Dame Press). He is co-editor of *Philosophy of Religion: Selected Readings* (Oxford University Press) and *Contemporary Debates in Philosophy of Religion* (Wiley-Blackwell). He served as General Editor of the Blackwell monograph series Exploring Philosophy of Religion and is founding Managing Editor of the journal *Faith and Philosophy*.

About the Series

This series explores problems related to God, such as the human quest for God or gods, contemplation of God, and critique and rejection of God. Concise, authoritative volumes in this series will reflect the methods of a variety of disciplines, including philosophy of religion, theology, religious studies, and sociology.

Cambridge Elements ⁼

The Problems of God

Elements in the Series

A full series listing is available at: www.cambridge.org/EPOG